Other books by Kellie R. Stone:
Are You out of Your Freakin' Mind? Break Mental Barriers and Live from Your Sacred Creative Space

Co-author of the International Best Seller:
Success In Beauty: The Secrets to Effortless Fulfillment and Happiness

Connect with Kellie:
WomensLifeLink.com
WomensLifeLink@gmail.com

The

Butterfly

Payoff

A Woman's Guide to Defining Her Purpose,
Fulfilling Her Dreams,
and Getting Paid for It!

Kellie R. Stone

LifeLink Publishing
Lexington, KY
WomensLifeLink.com
WomensLifeLink@gmail.com

Cover by Gruve Design Studio
Cover Photo by Elisabeth Zartl, ElisabethZartl.com

Illustrations by Cathy Lynn

The Butterfly Payoff: A Woman's Guide to Defining Her Purpose, Fulfilling Her Dreams, and Getting Paid for It!

By Kellie R. Stone—1st edition

ISBN-13:978-0692308882

DEDICATION

This book is dedicated to my mother, Linda Sue Kem. I know she felt as though she didn't fulfill her purpose before she died. Her feelings created a perspective that truly was just her own, though. To me, she was a good mom and a grandmother to my children—the most amazing and life-changing "purpose" a woman can ever have. Thanks for helping me become the woman I am today.

TABLE OF CONTENTS

Forward by Linda Joy..xiii
Introduction...xxi

PART I
UNDERSTANDING PURPOSE

Chapter 1   It's Your Journey.......................................1
Chapter 2   Cubic Zirconia Mentality in a
Diamond World.....................................9
Chapter 3   What Do You Want? 23
Chapter 4   What Can I Get YOU, Ma'am?.............39
Chapter 5   The Real Work Begins...........................43
Chapter 6   Bring In the Big Guns...........................51
Chapter 7   Purpose . . . Better Than Chocolate......61
Chapter 8   Listening To Your Authentic Self.........67
Chapter 9   Expanding Your Authentic Self............73

PART II
WHAT DREAMS MAY COME?

Chapter 10   Dream Seed..81
Chapter 11   Power To Change Things.......................91
Chapter 12   A Little Passion Goes a Long Way.......99
Chapter 13   Unforgiveness: A Major Roadblock...105
Chapter 14   Here Comes the Judge..........................111
Chapter 15   Choose Happiness-Choose Love........117
Chapter 16   Validation...125

TABLE OF CONTENTS

PART III
THE LIVING PAYOFF

Chapter 17   Seeing (Creating) It Through.............137
Chapter 18   It's all about YOU!...............................147
Chapter 19   The Body Payoff..................................151
Chapter 20   The Mind Payoff..................................159
Chapter 21   The Spiritual Payoff.............................167
Chapter 22   The Financial Payoff............................173
Chapter 23   The Ultimate Payoff: Knowing
              Yourself—Knowing Love....................185

BIOGRAPHIES

Kellie R Stone...200
Lisa Marie Rosati...204
Jan Deelstra..206
Sharon Nicholas..208
Alexa Linton..210
Charlotte Howard...212
Cathy Lynn..214
Bibliography...216

The Butterfly Payoff

ACKNOWLEDGMENTS

First, I would like to thank my family: Wally, Kori, Megan, Abbey, McKenna, Judah, and Lyric (and my fur babies) for giving me the support I've needed to complete this work, for sacrificing "mommy" time so I could brainstorm, write, and rewrite my ideas, for giving me the experiences that are the backbone of my message, for never making me feel guilty for being passionate about my dreams, and for loving me through all of my, sometimes, ugly and challenging transformation. You are all at the core of my life and, without you, I would not be who I am today.

For the special women with whom I'm so blessed to have crossed paths on my Journey (in no particular order): Tricia W., Vicky B., Elisabeth T., Kathy T., Jill S., Lisa Marie R., Sheri C., Jeffrie C., Linda J., Karin C., Donna M., Dawn D., Janet K., Jan D., Cheryl D., Tracey R., Denise H., Diane K., Ceal S., Nancy S., Stacey G., Terri H., Regina M., Lindsey D., Susy B., Sarah D., Ann B., Constance E., Kathy N., Candy S., Shilpa P., Deanna R. Terri T., Delise T., Angela J., Amy B., Sandy D., Leah H., Tricia D., Sandy B., and all the others who, for the moment, have slipped my mind, I thank you for connecting to me in ways that have filled my life with surprises, joy, tears, love, every emotion imaginable, and unbridled truth. Each of you, in your unique and beautiful ways, have taught me who I am, as well as who I am not.

Kellie R. Stone

I thank the empowered mentors and coaches I've had over the years and the ones who are still walking beside me now: Linda Joy, Lisa Marie Rosati, Christine Kloser, Brendon Burchard, Julia Cameron, Dr. Bradley Nelson, Christine McKenna, and Karin Coffey. You have changed my life in ways that are difficult to put into words, but know that your messages, dedication, and resolve to live your dreams has inspired me to work hard to ultimately become the grandest version of myself.

I thank you, Sandy, for being my therapist/confidant and for gently nudging me to always push myself farther than I think I can go. Thanks for listening to my rants, raves, and everything in between. Your support has made me a better woman, wife, mother, and messenger to women.

I thank all the teachers I've had along the way. Your classrooms were the havens of inspiration where I first realized that I had something to say and the tools to say it. Thanks for making me love the written word, for recognizing and encouraging my writing ability, and for always pushing me to do my best.

I am so very grateful to the women who graciously contributed their stories and artistic gifts to *Butterfly*. Lisa Marie Rosati, Alexa Linton, Sharon Nicholas, Jan Deelstra, Cathy Lynn, and Charlotte Howard, your wisdom, experiences, and understanding helped mold this project with deep rich clay that I could not have created without you. Muah!

My deepest gratitude to the gifted souls who helped

The Butterfly Payoff

make *Butterfly Payoff* a reality. Elisabeth Tilton, your formatting and design help is extraordinary. Mandy Gates, thanks for bringing the cover to life! Thank you so much to the talented Elisabeth Zartl for allowing me to use her beautiful photograph for the cover. Thanks, Bill Anderson Photography, for making me look so awesome in my head shot!

I thank the team of empowered women who have stepped up to the challenge of sharing pieces of themselves via my online-child, Womenslifelink.com. Terri H., Kori K., Elisabeth T., Cathy L., Lannah S., Tiffany R., Lisa Marie R., Priyanka C., Tricia W., Sandy D., Alexa L., Karin R., Angela S., Anca L., Heidi K., Donna M., Andrea A., Madeline W., Marta (Whitebook), Christina T., Henriette C., Jeffrie C., and all of you who have written guest posts, I am so honored to know you and am so thankful that you chose my community in which to share your beautiful thoughts and messages.

I thank the Women's LifeLink readers and participants for sticking with me even when I didn't want to stick with myself, for your input and contribution to the community as a whole.

I thank my clients for trusting in me and giving me the opportunity to serve you with my gifts. I am truly honored to be in your lives and a part of your self-development Journeys.

I am bowled over and in humble gratitude to my gifted mentor, Linda Joy, for investing your time to write the most heart-warming foreword I've ever read. Your sacred story and unwavering dedication to the women of this planet is inspiring and will always be at the forefront of my mind as I continue on a path to fulfill my sacred purpose and dreams. You are love in action.

With my whole being, I thank my awesome and completely loving God, the immense and inspiring Universe, the complex and all-embracing Mother Earth, and all the spiritual beings and masters that have influenced my life and showed me the stepping stones along my Journey.

And, lastly, I thank myself for pushing through a hellava lot to get here, for not believing everything I was told or that I thought about myself, for continually trying to be authentic . . . even when it hurts, for listening to my heart long enough to take a hint about my Purpose, Dreams, and the Payoff, for believing in Dreams and not giving up on them, for celebrating my gifts instead of hiding them. I love you.

FOREWORD

BY LINDA JOY

"When I shifted my focus away from the fear, I discovered that no matter how difficult the road ahead might look the thought of not living authentically and following my soul's purpose was far more frightening than the thought of moving forward."

As I sit on my deck on this glorious summer day, I find myself in awe of all of the butterflies flitting about my pond and garden. Talk about magical! It's like they know that I'm writing the foreword for Kellie's transformational book - *The Butterfly Payoff!*

When I think of life-altering change, I always picture an exquisite Monarch butterfly and remember the journey these mystical creatures endure to dance their brilliance in our gardens and fields.

The past twenty-four years have taken me on an amazing journey of self-discovery. I've moved through a rainbow variety of life experiences, some of which have filled me with intense joy and gratitude, and others which have pulled me into the deepest depths of self-doubt, pain, and despair. Like many women on the path of self-actualization, I have fallen—and yet, somehow, each time I have found that core of inner strength which helped me to struggle to my feet, brush myself off, and move on. In hindsight, I can see that what I previously perceived as my biggest mistakes have in fact been my truest and best lessons and my greatest gifts.

On the first leg of my journey, during which I went from high school dropout and runaway to single twenty-one year old welfare mom—oh, and let's not forget financial misfit—I had subconsciously labeled myself a failure. My mom dubbed me "the Queen of Self-Sabotage." When friends and family would ask me when I was going to do something with my life, I was prepared with a long list of reasons (which I now see were just excuses) why I didn't and couldn't and wouldn't have a chance at a life like that. I had spent so long viewing my life through a lens of shame and self-degradation that by the time I turned twenty-six I had already labeled myself a failure, and had turned my back on the dream of a better life.

It was a spring day in 1991 when the trajectory of my life was forever altered. In that one emotional, intimate and sacred moment sitting in my car on the side of the road I saw a glimpse into what my life could be like if I only I would allow it to be. That pivotal moment, which I write about in my bestselling anthology, A Juicy, Joyful Life, became the catalyst for me to take back my life, launch my quest to reclaim my authentic self and live my sacred purpose.

From that day forth, I spent every spare moment reading inspirational books from leading spiritual visionaries like Norman Vincent Peale, Florence Scovel Shinn, Napoleon Hill, and more. These authors became my virtual mentors. As the years unfolded, I added to my transformational toolkit, soaking up the wisdom of teachers like Louise Hay, Marianne Williamson, Debbie Ford, and Cheryl Richardson, to name a few. I surrounded myself with empowered, heart-centered women who had walked through fire to reclaim their authentic self. I dedicated myself to healing the cracked lens through which I viewed my life, so that I could create a better future for myself and my six-year-old daughter.

The written word became both my solace and my impetus for change. The wisdom contained within the books I chose seemed to come to me just when I needed it most.

Whether it was a word, a sentence, or a paragraph, each message that leaped off the pages at me was exactly what I needed to hear at that time, and gave me the fuel to move forward. To this day, I am grateful for visionary authors, like Kellie Stone, who continually step through their own fears and vulnerabilities to share their truth and bring their wisdom, insights, and gifts to the world. Each time someone shares their story and their truth, they become a beacon of light illuminating the path for others on the journey.

Kellie is one of those beacons of light!

I met Kellie in the midst of her healing and transform-ational journey that she so openly shares in the pages of *The Butterfly Payoff*. I saw her at her most wounded, and even then I could see her radiance, her desire to shed the layers of false stories and step into her full truth as a woman, a leader and a sacred guide to other

Kellie R. Stone

women on the journey. I saw, and held space, for her to see it in herself. As the 'reflector' – my role was to hold up the mirror so she could see her sacredness, wisdom, courage and spiritual gifts the same way I could. Her courage and commitment to owning her truth, stepping through her fears and sharing her soul-inspiring gifts with other women who are coming up the path behind her, continues to inspire me.

Today, Kellie is now the reflector for the women she serves in her thriving WomensLifeLink.com community, her work as a Women's Life Purpose Visionary/Inner Journey Strategist, and now through the pages of *The Butterfly Payoff.* Take the journey with Kellie through the pages of this book, complete the exercises that she guides you through and you'll discover that when you connect with your true passion, believe in yourself, and take inspired action to move forward, that only success can follow. On your journey you'll meet other inspiring women and read their stories of defining their purpose and fulfilling their dreams. Women, like my soul-sister Lisa Marie Rosati, who embodies authenticity and purposeful living, as well as Jan Deelstra and Alexa Linton whose stories will touch and inspire you.

I get soul giggles when I realize that my life has come full circle. Just as the written word empowered me to transform my life, today all of my multimedia brands are dedicated to publishing and producing the best in inspirational content to support women on their journey. From the queen of self-sabotage to the Publisher of Aspire Magazine – the premiere inspireational magazine for women, to the publisher of two best-selling books written by women and for women, as well as the founder of multiple inspirational brands each dedicated to inspiring, empowering, inspiring and supporting women in living deeper, more authentic and inspired lives —my winding journey has brought me to my purpose.

I now have the honor of working, collaborating and supporting many of the same leading visionaries whose books were an instrumental part of my personal and spiritual journey; including Louise Hay, Marianne Williamson, Debbie Ford, and many more light carriers. What gives me the greatest pleasure is partnering with and supporting some of today's up and coming movers and shakers in the fields of personal and spiritual development, natural living, success and conscious business —women like Kellie Stone!

In many media interviews over the last eight years, I've been asked how I have continuously stepped through my fears and out of my comfort zone to transform my personal, professional, and spiritual life. I can't offer any direct advice; I can only share my truth and what's worked for me. To move forward, I had to accept that change and transformation in our lives have the power to grip us in paralyzing fear—but only if we focus on the fear. When I shifted my focus away from the fear, I discovered that no matter how difficult the road ahead might look the thought of not living authentically and following my soul's purpose was far more frightening than the thought of moving forward.

Kellie R. Stone

A moment of enlightenment helped Kellie remember her purpose. In The Butterfly Payoff, Kellie courageously shares her transformational story along with several poignant stories of women who have found their ultimate purpose, mission and calling.

Kellie reminds us that change is sacred and deserves serious contemplation and time to manifest before moving on to the next big thing.

This transformational book is written with transparency, humor, encouragement and generosity. Within the pages you will find supportive visualizations, coaching exercises, energetic clearing meditations and a treasure trove of loving guidance. Being your beautiful self, remembering your authentic mission, and taking steps to live on purpose, is the fastest way to receiving *The Butterfly Payoff*.

My greatest wish for you is that you break free from your chrysalis, spread your beautiful wings and soar!

Live an Inspired Life!
Linda Joy
Bestselling Publisher,
Authentic Marketing Mentor & List Building
Expert AspireMag.net

The Butterfly Payoff

INTRODUCTION

"I only ask to be free. The butterflies are free."
– CHARLES DICKENS

I wrote this book for you—the woman who longs for the moment she understands who she is and why she is here. I have been her. Then I realized that my dreams and passions, my thoughts and talents, my abilities and creativity held the answer and key to remembering who I am. Yes, I did just say "remembering" not discovering. You see, I believe our spirits have an imprint of exactly who we are, a memory, though hidden from our conscious mind most of the time, waiting to be uncovered. This wonderful Journey on which we embark—The Journey to Purpose—is the path that reveals the mysteries about our sacred being and how to fulfill our highest Purposes.

It is my utmost Dream and Purpose to help you live the most fulfilling, juiciest, and purposeful life as the beautiful, delicious soul YOU are! And I have no doubt that you CAN do this! Many of you feel this intense appeal to answer prodding questions about who you are and why you are here, to fulfill your Dreams right now. Well, that's because we are the rising strength and hope for our world, for our species. We are the spiritual feminine essence of a planet that needs our love, nurturing, faith, joy, peace, brilliance, and creative energy. We can offer these gifts to our planet as a means to heal the wounds of our past and the present misuse and abuse of each other and the world. And, yes, this is an urgent call to you, to me, to every woman alive! Ultimately, I hope this book inspires the deepest part of your spirit and nudges you to keep moving forward and to always believe in yourself and your sacred, unique contribution to yourself and this world. Together, we can awaken from slumber and self-defeat and reach our highest Dreams. Now, here's a little peek into my inspiration for this book . . .

"How does one become a butterfly?" she asked. "You must want to fly so much that you are willing to give up being a caterpillar."
– FROM HOPE FOR THE FLOWERS

Think about a butterfly for just a minute. Picture one in your mind . . . the visual helps. Do you see how she (it could be a male, but this is a woman's book, so humor me) seems to be clueless and carefree as she flitters to her next destination? Picture the sudden flash of color, passing by at the strangest time, or an unexpected landing on your shoulder. Her delightful visit to the flowers in your garden presents a beautiful play unlike any other. All these events are seemingly contrary to the life of a creature with Purpose but, despite the flair for the spontaneous, butterflies fulfill their "thing" (reason for living) extremely well, do it looking pretty and get paid for it to boot—an example I am inspired by daily.

What if your life could be simply beautiful and carefree like hers? Impossible, right? What if I told you you're already a beautiful creature with the potential to be free, to be everything you can be? (I have to share the fact that a stunning yellow butterfly flew past me as I was writing this, nothing like a live object lesson and a literal confirmation.)

Our lovely flying friend's graceful dance (freedom to be nothing more and nothing less than what she is) intrigues us all. Butterflies symbolize hope, freedom, and profound metamorphosis—a creature bound to the land without wings when born, then transforms into a free flying wonder that moves through the air with ease, escaping the world that held her captive. A pretty good deal, don't you think?

I can hear you thinking: *What does my life have to do with a butterfly?* Truthfully, it has everything and nothing to do with it . . . let me explain.

> **At the deepest level of my soul, I believe that one of the most significant hindrances to true happiness and life-fulfillment for women is they don't know who they are, why they are here, and they don't have a clue how to figure these things out. I see the butterfly's life as an organic example of how beautiful and simple this process can truly be for us all.**

The Ancient Greek word for "butterfly" is ψυχή *(psychē)*, which primarily means *soul* or *mind*. An amazing coincidence? I don't think so. Could it be that, without all of the distractions we have today, the ancients saw something in those little winged creatures that served as an example of what they should remember about themselves? Our minds (*psyche* or butterfly) are powerful beyond measure. Awareness is just the beginning of each woman's unique flight path or Journey to Purpose. We all understand that the butterfly goes through immense changes to fulfill her destiny and become the beautifully designed creature she is. We are not so different, as the ancients proposed.

Butterflies instinctively travel for miles in a single day, seeking the simple things they need to live: sugar, salt, and water . . . oh, and a mate. Amidst that constant search for nourishment a truly astonishing thing happens: Purpose. Upon landing on those tiny flowers and plants, her feet attract pollen. Those life-giving particles are then transported via first class air to the next flower, where the little event known as pollination happens. So, what's the Payoff? Ask that butterfly if she's happy, full-bellied, and fulfilled . . . I bet she'll scream an emphatic, "YES!" Her **change** is inevitable. Her **purpose** is achieved. Her **reward** is created and experienced. It really is that simple. So, what do you say? Let's get started . . .

PART I
UNDERSTANDING PURPOSE

CHAPTER ONE

It's Your Journey

"We know that we determine our own destiny. We just have to take care of our own business, and we can't count on anybody else to do our work for us."
— BRIAN SHAW

My dear beautiful soul, I'm going to start by pointing out that four letter word up there in the sweet, little quote. I'm just going to come out and say it . . . WORK!

"I thought we were going to talk about flying free like butterflies, Kellie," you so adamantly say. Understand, I have a profound reason for talking about it first. When was the last time you went anywhere without some major planning and, let's face it, some work? My guess is, unless you have an all-purpose servant who does everything but carry you around in a royal rickshaw, you've broken a few nails, earned some gray hairs, and packed a few suitcases in your life.

We all love going on vacation, to the mall, or museum, right? For the most part all of these events are pleasurable and are considered worthy of working toward in our society. Our labor causes us to own those trips to the beach, to Nordstrom's, to the parent's hall of fame. We never complain about the "work" that's involved because there's a reward. I want you to think of your Life-Journey in the same way. Even that flitty-floaty butterfly takes care of her business. Remember, she does have a distinct Payoff, though. We must own the life we're given. No one can live it in our stead. No one will "do our work for us."

Have you ever met someone who whines about everything? She never accepts responsibility for her actions. Her pains and misfortunes are always the fault of someone else. It's fair to say that this perpetual victim mentality is precisely why she is living a life of despair and frustration. She has never realized that it's her Journey to own and treasure, to create. After all, isn't it much more fun to pass the proverbial buck on to Aunt Millie or anyone who willingly enables us to do so? For a while, perhaps, then it gets old . . . excruciatingly old.

A remarkable woman comes to mind. Her name is Helen Keller. Though everyone has at least heard of her, the story told in most text books and biographies may not make the point that I'm about to. Helen was someone who knew how to own her circumstances and make the best of the hand she had been dealt. Where so many get tripped up and fail, she succeeded. Why? I believe it was her circumstance of limited senses that gave her a unique perspective about **who she was and why she was here.**

She had no distractions (TV, radio, eye candy, social media, fussy kids) from the powerful emotions and drive she felt inside. Some of those emotions were dark, but only because she wanted to communicate so badly. Just think how many times we hesitate to speak out or be ourselves due to confusion, lack of confidence or fear. Not Miss Keller. Nothing stopped her from pushing (working) through her challenges to become one of the most renowned motivational icons of the twentieth century. She was an inspiration to all and not just to the physically-challenged—an astounding achievement for anyone. Like Helen, I tend to believe that our "limitations" are the key to making a distinct mark on the world. For it isn't usually what we have that makes us dig deeper for change, it's the inner Dream of the unmanifested that drives us. When we overcome lack or a situation, turn it into a positive serving element of our lives, we have used our restrictions to change something. In doing so, we may even change the lives of others like Helen did.

Consider the lot of her teacher/caretaker, Anne Sullivan, as well. How do you think she felt, responsible for a blind and deaf child, to be told to teach her without knowing if her technique would work? You bet she hurt inside, watching Helen struggle and throw temper tantrums. She could have easily given up, passed the job onto someone else. After all, Helen wasn't *her* child. No, Anne didn't do that. She owned her life, her Journey and, from it, pulled out every positive she could. For her dedication to her situation and Purpose, she earned a grateful student, a beloved friend and, together, they traveled to share their story and message with a world that needed to hear it. What is your message? Will you own it? Will you share it with the world?

It's easy to acknowledge all the pleasant things about our lives. We tend to grab hold of—with eager force—that which we've accomplished . . . call it pride. It's "I got a raise," or "I won the mom of the year award," or "I make the best turkey salad in the Midwest." However, look what happens when the tables are turned, when we discover a weakness, a flaw, or create some horrific mess that would strip us of all respectable status if others thought we were at fault: "The **devil** made me do it," or "**It** was a fluke," or "The **other driver** was going too fast." Maybe you've even said this: "Sorry, it's just **my personality** to be bossy and high strung." Not much accountability there, huh? Well, I'm here to tell you, it's all the same deal, the same life, the same you, regardless of your circumstances. *YOU* created it! Own it!

Okay, I promised you a profound reason for even mentioning *Work* so soon. Here it is. Are you ready? No, I mean *really* ready. You might want to sit down for this one.

With every action there is a reaction.

Forgive me for the trip back to fifth grade science class. Old school or not, it's the truth. The truth you need to hear. I didn't write this book to make you feel good or to tell you that the world can be yours, that you can fly free like the butterfly without lifting a finger. If you want to Journey to Purpose, action is required . . . did I mention this is an interactive book? The first "action" is for you to accept your life as your own and stop making excuses for your failures and mistakes. Don't worry, these "boots were made for walking," so to speak. You'll get that one later.

More Purpose than One

On my Journey I've discovered two types of Purpose: Individual and Collective Contribution (or sacred Purpose). Individual Purpose is that which you chose at a soul level to experience in order to complete a personal set of goals; such as, overcoming character flaws and mistakes, growing in love and compassion, and experiencing certain emotions. I've seen this type of Purpose in play for my entire life. It is the directive that often creates difficulty and challenges that, while going through them, make you wonder what the hell is happening and what you did to deserve this. Yes, I think we've all experienced times like these. Why would we choose to create moments of pain? Well, because it's what our souls need in order to know ourselves and to ascend to higher spiritual levels. But it's not all suffering with individual Purpose. It is also enlightenment and experiencing our greatest potential.

Do you ever feel like you come back to the same character development scenarios over and over again? If so, this may indicate that you are dealing with an individual Purpose plan that hasn't quite been mastered. This is extremely common and can bring about the most fulfilling times of your life, as you embrace the change you've set out to conquer. If you are not ready to tackle this Purpose, you won't. It will remain there until you are ready to make the appropriate changes and develop the areas it represents. This process is more organic and does not always require us to consciously understand it all to work in our lives. However, there is truth to be learned and embraced with our individual Purposes. I personally choose to understand myself at the core, to dig deeper for reasons things happen and for satisfying solutions. I also know that individual Purpose helps to prepare and equip us for our Collective Contribution Purpose.

Oh, to have a grand Purpose that would change the world! Well, guess what? YOU HAVE ONE! We all have one. They may not all seem grand in the world's terms, but they are all necessary and do, indeed, change the lives of others and the world as a whole. Collective Contribution is Purpose you choose on a soul level that helps to complete a larger agenda—one that affects us all. Truly understanding what your sacred Purpose is one of the most satisfying things you will ever do because it allows you to put into practice all of the individual Purpose you've been working on for so long.

This collective agenda carries weight universally in that it is a master plan that never compromises with standards and results. In other words, it keeps on going until the desired result is in place—sort of how I want you to work toward your Purpose and Dreams. Part of this work is the revelation that you are important just as you are now and are already changing the world. What further projects you wrap yourself around are completely your choice and will play out when you are ready. This is a Journey—one that requires patience, trust, belief, hope, faith, forgiveness, and all the love we can assemble. Shine brightly and be strong in all that you do as you Journey to and through Purpose.

CHAPTER TWO

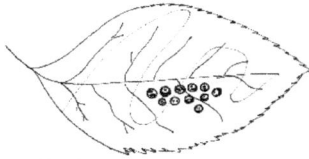

Cubic-Zirconia Mentality in a Diamond World

"Better a diamond with a flaw than a pebble without."

– CHINESE PROVERB

When a woman wears a real diamond, she markedly changes her posture, her confidence, and the way she carries herself. This is an interesting observation that deserves a couple of laps around our brains . . . you know, for the sake of understanding something about ourselves. Why do you think a stone can make such a difference in our perceived self-worth and attitude? Besides the fact that it's all pretty and sparkly. OK, now for the real reasons. One is psychological and the other is scientific.

#1 – Wearing something valuable does not make us valuable. Truth is, we feel better about ourselves when we touch or possess something valuable or authentic. This is nothing more than our human ego at play. Put a glass rock on the same gal, and tell her it's glass, she won't experience the same euphoria as she does with the genuine diamond. (That last statement, a no brainer but not this next one.)

#2 – All substances in the universe have unique vibrations or frequencies. (I told you it was scientific.) Diamonds happen to be one of those substances that live at the higher end of the vibration scale, as do most gemstones and precious metals. Our energy resonates with the energy of authentic matter from nature and, in turn, resonates with ours. Hmmm . . . where do you think I'm going with this? I'm talking about our state of being. Are you acting like diamonds and vibrating with your authentic frequency (all shiny and sparkly) or are you faded, lackluster, like a piece of cut glass?

Here's another example: (You fashionistas out there will appreciate this one) Most women know of iconic fashion brands like Coach®, Dolce & Gabbana®, Chanel®, and so forth. Well, as much as most women would love to own just one of those designer handbags, the majority may not be able to afford such luxuries. So, what do we do? Buy a knock-off. Simple. And, before we know it, the twenty bucks we spent might as well have been thrown out the window. That cheap look-alike starts unraveling, losing its buttons or snaps, and the zipper breaks. It may look like the real deal, but it can't perform in the same way, withstand constant use or fool those who have the real thing.

Now, here's the application: I'm guessing you are living a life that is not quite as authentic and dynamic as you'd like, otherwise, you wouldn't be reading this. Most women are too busy fooling themselves into believing they are happy and fulfilled with their twenty-dollar-knock-off life. Sorry, for being harsh, but I told you I'm not messing around with your Life-

Journey. I'm here to help you find your way. If it makes you feel better, I have had a knock-off life (and purses), too.

Finding the Authentic

It's crucial to discover your authentic self before your buttons start popping and your zipper breaks. Seriously. Our bodies break down if we don't find joy, peace, love, Purpose, and just enjoy our lives. If you are skeptical, let me share a little story with you that might change your mind.

A Circle Can't Be Square (My Experience)

There was a time in my life I now refer to as the "dark ages" for reasons you will understand after reading this account. I had my fifth child in the late 1990s. I'd like to say that I enjoyed the pregnancy and everything was peachy, but it wasn't. After experiencing tremendous back pain and sciatica during the last month of carrying him, I finally gave birth to a healthy, nearly nine-pound boy. That was the enjoyable part. The trouble came after. My marriage was strained, my body hurt, and I didn't have a clue about why my life felt so empty. After all, I was a mom of five beautiful children, had a good man and was active and respected in my community and church. Aren't all those things wonderful and shouldn't they have fulfilled me? Let me just say, it was one of those WTF moments we all have from time-to-time.

Though, up to that point, I had played on the banks of the river called, serving-the-greater-good-of-mankind and embracing my reason for being here, I still had not wholly jumped in and let it carry me to the fulfilling life I envisioned and was born to live. I wanted some answers but, unfortunately, I didn't know where to look. Yes, I prayed. I cried. I took classes. I even started businesses. None of those things pointed me fully in the right direction. Though, they did fill me with experience I would later use.

During the dark ages, I was diagnosed with Fibromyalgia and was extremely depleted of vital nutrients. Change was inevitable . . . or I would slip further into my oblivion. My own illness prompted me to research natural wellness and carry out what I thought was the best course of action for me. My health became my focus and my Purpose . . . or so I thought. I remember taking handfuls of vitamin and mineral supplements daily to combat the condition and my chronic fatigue. My actions made a difference in how I felt physically, but I wasn't addressing the other, more elusive, facets of health. Mental and emotional issues rose up and bit me in the ass—hard. Again, I was forced into a lonely corner where I asked, "Why?"

A series of tragic events unfolded, exacerbating my poor situation. In fact, I was emotionally incapacitated. After caring for my cancer-riddled mother for fourteen months and watching her die, losing my thirty-four-year-old brother to a bizarre strep virus, and discovering my grandfather's three-day-old dead body in a hot house, I could not go on as the woman, the mother, the wife I had worked so hard to become. Life had dealt me the crappiest hand anyone could imagine. I was lost, emotionally alone, and begging for answers. I'm going to tell you the *whole* truth: I lost it! I was a basket case! Faking my way through life.

I'm not looking for sympathy here. I just want to make a strong point you won't forget easily. So, allow me to tell you the rest of the story. I had reached a point where no supplements, no amount of sleep, and no friendly advice (layman or professional) made any difference to my body or my mind. Chronic illness had set up camp. My dear family doctor then diagnosed me with Chronic Migraine Disease, Chronic Daily Headache, and with the proverbial stick that broke the camel's back: Clinical Depression. I suffered immensely through the pain and isolation that came with spending days and weeks in bed and drugged up with narcotics or other strong meds. True help evaded me, and I was in no condition to sort through the underlying causes of my demise.

Eventually, I did see some improvement with anti-depressant medications, but they altered my perception of life. I contracted a case of the "whatevers" and waltzed through my days not really caring much about anything. Wait, there's more.

After losing a family business, I was forced back into the job market, regardless of my health. I believe I was in denial at that point and really just wanted to escape. I had trained in the interior design field, had always been extremely creative, and consistently worked well in sales positions. Naturally, I tried to get something utilizing some or all of those skills. Nothing was opening up for me, so I visited a previous employer whom I had worked for as a designer years before. The only thing she had open was a position in the office. Desperately needing money and to end my search, I took the position. Don't get me wrong, sometimes you have to do things that don't necessarily fit your best qualifications, but going too far against your personality/purpose grain leaves you with splinters not easily removed. I found that out the hard way.

Regardless of the lack of creative stimulation, I was excited about my new job that, at least, allowed me to work near my beloved design world. Well, sort of, if you call sitting at a desk in a cluttered backroom for eight to nine hours a day involved in design. The job liked me, though, as I excelled in keeping the order. I enjoyed being needed and the fact that things ran better than they had before I got there. What I didn't like was my stifled creative juices and no real time with people—two things that made me (the authentic gal) happy.

Consequences for Not Living Authentically

Ignoring my soul cry to make a change, I stayed at the position for well over a year. My mood and physical health declined even further right before everyone's eyes (recall, I already had Fibromyalgia, Migraine disease, Chronic Daily Headache, and Depression under my belt). Creative and outgoing, as I had always been, I still chose to ignore the child-like need to express an inseparable part of myself. Becoming angry and stressed, I ended up in the hospital with more bills, more meds and quite without a job. I paid for that one for a long time. Stick with me here, as I will share my enlightenment with you later in the book.

The major point to my little trip down memory lane is this: Pay attention to how you spend most of your time, asking, *Does what I am doing give me energy or does it drain me? Do I like who I am when I'm doing it?* We all have the same 24-hours a day, and many of us spend nearly half of those hours working for a living. Something you do so much can have a huge impact on the woman you think you are and the one you become. Just take an inventory of your day and see how much time you spend on various activities. I know this exercise will enlighten you. As you learn more about the person you are and aren't, you will know what changes need to happen in this area. A good friend and fellow light worker, Dr. Tricia Working, believes in discovering the best version of yourself and recently encouraged women with these words: *"Let's not waste time on conditions, situations and even people who do not enhance and enrich our lives."* Her message is so clear but, unfortunately, not always easy to adhere to. She went on to say, *"Our spirits are so much stronger than those things which intrude upon us, so let us have our daily lives blend into a life we choose, not one thrust upon us."*

Getting this now will change your life forever. If you have children, then you remember the toy puzzle that requires fitting wood shapes into corresponding holes. It remains one of my favorite life-lesson tools. Did you ever watch a child struggle endlessly to fit the square into the circle, or the diamond into a rectangle upon his first attempt to solve the puzzle? Frustrating, huh? Eventually, the child gets it right, waits until coordination improves, or just abandons the source of annoyance all together. Don't do the same thing with your life unnecessarily.

Stop trying to be a square when you're a circle. Discover who you are, what you are meant to do, and fill the hole in which *YOU* fit. If that means foregoing a life in business to stay at home with your babies, then DO IT! On the other hand, if it means the bored housewife needs to go back to school to learn how to teach French, then SO BE IT! Jan Deelstra, a powerful self-esteem specialist and transformational author, also had first-hand experience with a rough road to discovering her authentic, fulfilling path. Her story testifies to how spending too much time outside of your whole truth can make life treacherous and even harmful.

Jan Deelstra's Story:

Ten years working in the trenches of the Department of Human Services is too long to be immersed in societal ills. I became jaded, if not chronically cynical. In addition to being privy to every vile imaginings of human conditions, my job duties also placed me in a position to supervise Graduate School interns. It wasn't

until one of those interns, Margaret, brought to my attention my own warped perspective, compelling me to consider the consequences of too many years of working in such a supposedly diverse arena.

Margaret was a traditional mother and housewife who, having raised her children, decided to return to graduate school. She was devout in her religious affiliation and, although sheltered personally from the street mire, she was unusually bright and well-versed in the ways of the world. First blush had her pigeonholed as a Stepford-type robotic wife: The little woman who lived by the outlandishly sexist tenets of Fascinating Womanhood. However, that initial biased observation would prove to be the antithesis of the Margaret I came to know and respect.

As time passed and her internship went on, I watched Margaret's true colors seep forth in full-spectrum. She was a woman of conviction, but her convictions did not blind her to the subjective plight of the clientele. Her unhesitant full-plunge into the social sludge was as impressive as a Mormon Pioneer— elbow deep in a garden fertilized with ox manure. Margaret made home visits into the bowels of so-called civilization, bravely treading where the fringe and even roaches barely survived. She raised funding for infant and toddler caskets when mortality won. She corralled prissy senators and legislators and sought out media personnel in hopes of shining the light on the darkest of social issues. She co-conducted self-awareness groups and fiercely rallied the wagons to protect from budget cuts those programs which were constantly in the crosshairs of conservative knife-wielding politicians.

Margaret was the best of the best interns. She did a great job. And I like to believe she learned much as a result of her immersive internship. But in the end, as it often is, it was this teacher who learned the most.

On her last day, Margaret's words (more than the elfin-sized poetry book she handed me) were her parting gift to me. Purposefully and patiently she waited until I looked squarely at her intense face. I sensed something just shy of dire was about to be bared.

"The rest of the world is not all like this," she said looking deeply into my eyes. "The rest of the world is not all like this," she enunciated as my nonchalant nod was not well enough connected to her sentiment. Clearly, Margaret wanted to be certain I had grasped the magnitude of her carefully crafted words. It was then that I understood. Margaret was not about to leave the internship program until I had learned my lesson: The rest of the world is not all like this.

What Margaret was telling me was that I had begun to see the entire world as broken, dys-functional, drama-infused, addicted, heartless, hopeless, and nefarious. And, she was right. She called me out on my jaundiced perspective. All of the teachings I communicated about our biases affecting our view of our world experience, of how all conversation is tainted with projections, all of my instructions to Margaret, to my clients, and to the past interns were in my face in one brutally profound sentence: "The rest of the world is not all like this."

Her parting words resonated deep within me, and with a resounding truth that circled for months before finally settling into my grey matter. The job was killing me or, at very least, I was tainted and world-worn. Even as Margaret's words swirled, I began to look for the light . . . the one that wasn't a train coming at me. In earnest, I looked for my cartoon escape hatch. The gig was up. The joke was on me. I'd overstayed my welcome. All the clichés lined up. I'd look and then I'd leap. Out with the old . . .

Margaret was my last intern. I opened a small gift shop, Ruby Luna's Angel Emporium, and made my escape from social work. In my estimation, the first half of my life had been hard, and I consciously vowed that the next half would be fun and rewarding.

A funny thing happened on the way to change: Customers of Ruby Luna's were seeking something. They may have been looking for an angel lapel pin to protect them from whatever perceived evil lurked, or they may have fallen in love with the cherub shower curtain. They may have giggled at whimsy or, perhaps, they were inspired to purchase a celestial statue, a gossamer dress, a beautiful otherworldly CD, an angelic journal, or a greeting card for someone in mourning. Along with the subjective searches for wares came a story . . . always, there was a story of loss or love, of healing, or of miracles and synchronicities. And there I was again, immersed in societies' heroic and/or horrific stories and, still, being that listening consultant, often advising, albeit in a much more pleasant venue.

Margaret was right. "The rest of the world is not all like this." The whole is not as fractured as was the sampling of either my Human Services caseload or my angel store customers, as both microcosms are tainted by intensity of settings and content and even demographics.

Although, at the time, when I opened the Angel Emporium, I didn't realize that in both circumstances I was providing a service designed to help and hopefully enlighten and empower. Twenty-twenty retrospection completely blurs the fact that I opened the angel store because I adore Victorian design, and angels and cherubs are a big part of that interior design theme. I had believed I was opening an angel store because I could make a living selling the interior tabletop kitsch that I so loved to surround myself with. What better way to get the wares at wholesale than to open a store! It seemed the furthest distance from the fox holes I had survived . . . Silly me. I was only recreating a place where others would gather to mend. And, in the end, it was a wonderful thing.

Following the death of my son, I had no more to give to grieving customers and, once again, I planned my escape and moved to Southern California to heal and write through my own losses. Eventually, I exited the study of my stories, and I came out from within with a roar.

So much brilliant light lit my way and, suddenly, I knew exactly why I was born. All those stories, all those experiences were the necessary rungs on my ladder that led to my authentic calling. Actually, I was always living my calling. I just hadn't recognized it as such.

Now that I've moved my consulting business from the walls of brick and mortar and into the ethers, I see so many similarities in the whole of the planet's inhabitants. Humans are awakening, and this was evidenced in both the social work position and the celestial proprietress position. The awakening is greater now, and even though I am no longer seeking the means to buy tiny caskets and no longer visit drug havens, searching for a signature of parental consent so that my teenaged-mother-client might receive medical help, and I am no longer surrounded by shelves full of angels, moons, suns, and stars, I am still, perhaps more than ever, surrounded by the light.

It is this light that I share on my website, through my books and articles and classes and products and services. It is the light that I hope you'll share, too. Together, we create magnificent timeless and endless ripples at a time in history when the Universe is calling us to awaken.

Take a deep breath after that beautiful story. Jan's enlightening experience so vividly paints a picture of her truth and Purpose for not only her to recognize but to release it fully to a world to which she had already selflessly connected herself. All of life's steps are important, even when they are painful and confusing. I love how Jan realized that she had been journeying on a path that led her right to her ultimate calling. Let us all be this aware and flexible.

CHAPTER THREE

Where Do I Start?

"There's an old Chinese proverb that says the journey of a thousand miles begins with a single step. If a woman can make simple pledges to change the small things, she's well on her way to leading a fuller, healthier life."

– FLORENCE HENDERSON

If someone had told me, when I was eight, that I'd someday write a book and quote Florence Henderson (Mrs. Carol Brady), there surely would have been laughter . . . much laughter. No disrespect of her at all. I just didn't see her as a philosopher at the time. I much preferred Alice for that sort of thing.

Let's take a look at Florence's key phrases:

"The journey of a thousand miles

begins with a single step."

AND

". . . make simple pledges to change . . ."

Translation: Take it slowly or you'll be sorry. Too many women experience goal-reaching burn out while striving to fulfill important Dreams. **Why do they give up so easily? Why do they let circumstances get in the way of being who they are or obtaining what they want?** It's fairly simple: They often take on too much all at once. Eat the elephant too quickly and you get indigestion. Stick to the "one bite at a time" theory.

I know this woman well. She gets all excited about the end result and does everything she can to MAKE IT HAPPEN. It's an adrenaline spike, a conscious decision that usually cannot last the course. How do I know this? I am one of those women. I've had to be extremely careful about doing too much too quickly. Change is sacred and deserves serious consideration, enough so that we give it time to manifest and get settled before we move on to the next challenge. Purpose is found in many places, many actions, many relationships but, most of all, it's found *within* you, right where you stand, as Jan discovered.

Are You Ready for Purpose?

Have you ever been shopping for a specific item like a formal dress or pair of shoes? Well, sure you have. And, while on that shopping trip, did you tend to get really distracted by all the new seasonal fashions and trends. Suddenly, your purposeful trip to the mall gets derailed . . . at least for a few minutes while you rush to the dressing room to try on that cute top you just can't resist. After all, it's so much fun to indulge in things that don't have rhyme or reason, huh? And, though I have my fair share of these carefree occasions, I want to use this scenario to explain how living your life like this regularly can literally derail your train to authentic Purpose.

I've realized on my own Journey to Purpose that not every woman is ready to even think about why she is here, let alone what that truly means. The question, "Are you ready for Purpose?" deserves an answer. Understand, that it's perfectly fine, once you understand your Purpose, to set the serious stuff aside for a season so it can simmer and mature. However, if you are ignoring it all together, you may find yourself struggling needlessly. If life is difficult and lackluster, it could be a sign that you are not listening to your inner goddess—the lovely inner self who doesn't like it too much when she doesn't get her way. Her way is the higher way . . . just so you know. Hearing her takes some courage and open mindedness because you know things will likely need to change a little after that heart-to-heart.

The Beauty of Passion and Talent

Every day your gifts, talents, and passions surround you. They are affixed to who you are and likely won't disappear unless you flat out refuse to engage in them. And, trust me, I'm not saying that you should push any of those things out of your life. But, I do want you to pay attention to how those qualities serve you and others, how they progress, and how they fit into your life Dreams. Sometimes passion and talent show up in ways that don't lead you directly to your authentic Purpose. In those instances they can actually distract you from the very thing you are meant to do. I have the perfect example:

Years ago, before I knew what my Purpose was, I started writing a novel . . . a paranormal, crime thriller to be exact. I know, right? Pretty far away from what I do now. Anyway, I really loved it and was passionate about every word I typed. I even thought I'd found my true career path. I was fine with being a novelist for the rest of my life . . . really. The process of finishing my first novel was a lot of work but more satisfying than anything I'd done career wise in the past. It was a beautiful thing. Well, that was until I started feeling unfulfilled and as though something important was missing.

I struggled with it for a while, pushed the buttons when clearly I wasn't supposed to. Don't get me wrong, it all had a reason for showing up in my life . . . I believe **Purpose is the child of reason**. Luckily, I recognized the subtle messages from within and from beyond myself, and I accepted that my career as a novelist would not take center stage. Maybe I would allow it to be in an off Broadway, side show . . . *wink, wink*.

Now, even though I have days when I would love to just be a novelist, I know that beautiful talent was a mere stepping stone to get me writing again and digging a little deeper into what I would use it for. So, the bottom line: though passion and talent is beautiful and amazing, it doesn't always mean you should glue yourself to it for the long haul. Experience it, be grateful for it, but allow it to carry you further into Purpose and regular communication with the goddess and outside divine influence.

Clarity . . .

At Last

Seeing something clearly is extremely validating and fulfilling . . . not like the confusing, broken feeling I get in the morning while trying to read my phone screen without my glasses. When we are able to focus completely on something, we are at our best—our highest functioning. Multitasking really is overrated. When we allow ourselves to push closer to the authentic being who craves attention, we are able to release that which no longer serves and can clutter our lives.

Clarity of Purpose is the mother-load of satisfaction. It shows you who you are and what steps will bring that woman to the forefront of your life— the woman who serves the world with her personal best. The energy that surrounds you while staying on the Journey to Purpose is literally electrifying! Life becomes easier. People and opportunities show up out of the blue. It serves you to remain faithful to this path. You may also find that those other passions and talents fit in nicely, even if they look a little different.

This focusing stuff is really a way of learning how to listen to your gut, your intuition. We, as women, should never leave this part of ourselves behind for anything or anyone. The more we connect to our goddess, the more she illuminates the path ahead. This kind of focus and clarity is how those famous, balanced, world-shaking women made it to their truth and authentic place in the world. I have another beautiful example of how gifts and passion can transform into a purposeful life. My dear colleague, Charlotte Howard, recently shared what she found on the stepping stones to the fulfilling life she now leads.

Charlotte Howard's Story

Have you ever wondered if you have the strength to pursue your dreams, passions and purpose? I did! What held me back? Fear! Fear of what others would think of me. Fear of not succeeding. I'm not the only one. Fear holds so many women back in life. It is my hope that my story helps empower you to be everything you want to be.

As a teenager, I was raped and felt like my life was worthless. I tried to overdose on pills, hoping all the bad memories would go away. I didn't even tell my mom until ten years later because I was afraid of what others would think of me. What held me together during this trying time? Having faith in God and believing in myself. This was the first step forward on my life journey.

After the rape, I knew I didn't want any other woman to reach a point in her life where she did not want to go on because of feelings of worth-lessness. It was that moment when I decided to pursue a journey to empower women to unlock their own beauty from the inside out. My journey did, however, start in a different way. I went to cosmetology school right after high school and earned my degree. I worked in a corporate beauty salon for over a decade as an award-winning hair stylist/manager until I had to walk away from my career. But, understand, I did not abandon my passion.

I know you are probably wondering what changed. Why would I leave a job that I enjoyed? Though, I was gifted at my job, like many women, I wanted to pursue my passion, purpose and dreams at deeper levels. Not to mention, the long 70 to 80 hour work weeks in this environment unfortunately caused Carpal Tunnel Syndrome—a condition I could not overlook. In beauty school, they taught me everything I needed to know to provide hair and beauty services, but they did not teach me how to take care of my mind, body and soul.

My doctor demanded that I find a new profession. I asked, "Are you kidding me?" I loved what I did, but it made me think deeply about my health and future. I knew I had to make a change quickly. And, I knew my kids needed their mommy to be healthy and happy. I began to evaluate things I could do that would allow me to still pursue my journey while I finalized my time working in corporate America.

After talking it over with my family and taking inventory of my expenses and savings, I took a leap of faith and started my life coaching and consulting business for women. I became very successful at empowering women to pursue their passion, purpose and dreams. I also empowered women to boost their confidence, self-esteem, and beauty from the inside out. That was the year 2000. Since then, I have expanded my businesses with an international radio show, magazine, products, and services that cater to heart-centered women who are mostly moms.

Is success without fulfillment really success at all? This was a question I asked myself. I believe happiness is the soul of success. If you are at peace with the choices you have made and are content with the way life has turned out, you most definitely are more successful than most people you know. Success, for me, is not necessarily achieving every goal I've set, but it's how enriched I am while striving to achieve it. Don't shun your mistakes. Take them into stride because these are valuable life lessons. In hindsight, they are golden words of advice thrown at you by life itself.

Think about how your definition of success was formed. Was it in your upbringing, beliefs, traits, attitude, priorities in life, peers, family, society, and the things you have been through in life? Can you make the connection? Sure you can! But, are you positive this is the definition you want to stick with? I am talking about reinvention and finding a new you here. Understand that it is okay to make changes.

There is a myth that says people are born winners or born losers. Nothing could be further from the truth. Yes, there are techniques, methods, and ways of behaving that enable and empower us to succeed. Certain attributes determine whether you will succeed or not. But these are not attributes you need to instill. We all have loads of them already. All we need is a little clarity of thought and, voila: the revelations rain in!

The foremost attribute I'm speaking about is self-motivation. If you are not self-enthused you won't put your heart and soul into the cause. To achieve anything, you have to put all 100% of yourself out there.

Secondly, having a *flexible* and *clear approach* to situations broadens your horizon. There are some things that are just beyond our realm until we reach for them. If you accept this fact and move on to better things in life, success becomes so much simpler.

And, lastly, a tinge of *faith* and *eternal hop*e gets you through all those snags and hitches that keep you away from tasting sweet success. If you feel that life hasn't been fair with you, don't lose hope. It's never too late to make a stint in the marathon called life. Your engine just needs a little revving up! You have come to the right place!

Consider a postage stamp. Its usefulness consists of the ability to stick to one thing till it gets to its destination. Sticking to your purpose in life is the catch. How many times have you joined the gym and never went back after the first week? How many times you have job hopped?

Kette R. Stone

All you need is clarity of thought and the world will be your oyster!

What is your life all about? Do you let events happen to you rather than go out and make them happen? If you know where you are going in life, you automatically feel good about yourself. As you gain control of your life, confidence comes. Happiness infuses your spirit. I know where I'm going in life: deeper into my purpose. What do you really want out of life? Seek the answer within yourself, in your changed perception of success, and in your mission statement, while pursuing your personal journey.

Write down this personal vision and mission statement. It brings the clarity I'm talking about. This statement is essentially your road map to destination-life! Upfront this exercise might seem unnecessary but, as you experience it, you realize that you may be behind in your personal dreams. It will give you direction and momentum to move forward. Remember that everyone and everything in life has a purpose. Live and learn and be clear about your perception of the future because that's where will spend the rest of your life!

*Now, let me ask you again . . .
Are you ready for Purpose?*

Location, Location, Location

I need to be clear about something. If you don't know *where* you are, moving into new life-success can be scary and confusing. It's imperative that you understand your placement in the various areas of your life. You have to be willing to look at the big picture, even if it's ugly and bears no resemblance to what you desire it to be. This big picture will give you the location of your body, mind, and spirit. It will ultimately be your ground zero—the preparatory place from which you will reconnect to your Journey to Purpose and start creating and experiencing the Payoff.

Remember Dorothy on the yellow brick road? There was a distinct starting point (the swirly thingy) where she and little Toto began their long trip to the Emerald City. Knowing where she was enabled her to feel more confident about her challenging Journey. And, think about how many really cool characters and places she encountered along the way. Her destination wasn't the big deal she thought it was. It was her Journey that changed her life and attitude about who she was and where she belonged—her Purpose. We all have a "yellow brick road." Will you let me help you find it?

In all honesty, I've forsaken this step many times for fear of acknowledging how bad things were. However, once I decided to move beyond the past and get serious about my future by living in the present, I could no longer use this as an excuse to lounge in a private cesspool of denial. I realized it was okay to be where I was. I accepted my state, my darkness, and allowed it to be okay. With that discovery came freedom to execute a new plan for my future (a small tidbit of my renaissance). There was, however, another ingredient in my self-destructive omelet: procrastination. I put off what hurt, shocked, and cost me something much too great to give up (still do sometimes). Sound familiar? I know I'm not alone. All humans do this on occasion. But, you should know, it's not the occasional putting off of a chore that brings you to a standstill, it's the *chronic laziness*, the *habitual behavior* that gets you into trouble. It's interesting how those two phrases even sound degrading and send your mind into a negative tailspin. Enough of that darkness, let's move into the light.

The best way to get a clue about your personal location is to rate each area of your life. This is easily done. And you don't need fancy equipment, expensive therapy, or multiple medications to do it. It's just a simple number rating system that anyone can use. I know most of you have fallen for those online surveys that promise you some big prize upon completion. They ask you about a thousand questions and want you to rate your favorite products on a scale from zero to ten. After the fifth page, you normally give up and think no prize is worth all of that thinking. Well, if you can endure even one page of that, you can do this. Here is a list of the ten general areas of life in no particular order of importance.

Finances: This is your general financial state overall that includes your income, investments, bank account, reserve, and your ability to manage them.

Physical Health: Think in terms of your body and its current state of health.

State of Mind: The most difficult to change but the most satisfying, the mindset is how you view your world, how you process information, and what you believe about yourself and others.

Purpose/Contribution: This is your special talents, giftings, and callings and how you apply them to life on the planet. If you don't know what your unique attributes are, then consider how you give into your family, community, and/or world.

Business/Career: Your life outside of home and personal relationships, your work, business, and any path to uphold it, such as, education and expanding your knowledge.

Social: This is your time spent with others outside of family and work. All social encounters and engagements. This includes friends, extended family, and social media.

Fun/Recreation: The time you spend enjoying life with others or alone. This includes hobbies, vacation time, self-care and any time when you are not on the clock . . . at home or the office.

Primary Relationship: Your relationship with your significant other.

Family: This can include immediate and extended

family relationships.

Spiritual: Your spiritual path that is unique to you. Consider your sense of a higher being or collective consciousness and how you view topics like God, prayer, mediation, enlightenment, inner growth, etc.

The easiest way for me to explain this is to use the "product" rating example from above. Pretend you have been asked to prioritize these ten products in the order of importance to you. After you've taken some time to evaluate what has the most significance in your life, rate your level of satisfaction with each one? Would one be a ten and another a four? This is a personal survey of your life only *you* can complete . . . remember, it's your Journey. When you are finished, your life areas are listed in the order of importance to you.

It might look something like this:

1. Spiritual—7

2. Primary Relationship—5

3. Family—7

4. Physical Health—5

5. State of Mind—4

6. Finances—3

7. Contribution—2

8. Business—4

9. Fun/Recreation—4

10. Social—7

This exercise not only gives you a personal GPS coordinate for each part of your life, but it compartmentalizes that which can be overwhelming if grouped together. One of the biggest, most common mistakes made when facing adversity and challenge or trying to improve life is to focus on everything all at once. You know those really LONG "to do" lists that never quite get finished? They almost always get tossed or remain in journal-purgatory indefinitely. Keep your "life area" list in a safe place. You'll need it later. For now, I want you to focus on just one of those life areas: State of Mind. Even if you've categorized it as the least important it needs some immediate attention. Before anything else changes, you must change your mind (this is your metamorphosis).

Generally, people tend to dwell on problems when they get bad enough to create something uncomfortable or change the present lifestyle. The mind is obsessed with finding the answers to the riddles that seem endless sometimes. Doing this for long periods of time is what solidifies the mindset. It's a pattern of thinking and the way in which we look at our lives and the situations represented there. It's how we measure ourselves and our ability to either transcend, stay the same or fall back. Mindset is the authority by which we live.

It takes guts to examine our minds on a level that may expose weakness and darkness. To face who you have become because of what you think can be scary and difficult if there are monsters of negativity and skeletons of past pain lurking around the corners of your mind. It's easy to see why fear often prevails in the challenge to transform our lives, to reach the summit of our Dreams. I believe that, no matter how deeply your mind is involved with the setbacks of the past, you can achieve your goals with a little push and the appropriate tools. Take a good long look at your mindset and see what might be holding you back from your heart's desire. What beliefs and ideas might be standing in your way?

Many of these thoughts and feelings about yourself and your ability to secure the life of your dreams may come from old habits and long ago statements made to you by others. But until you search the dark recesses of your mind, you won't uncover the entrance to your yellow brick road, the path to your Payoff. And, let me tell you, it is a lifetime of discovery, purging, and rebuilding a more serving thought life. Just remember that you are in charge here. You hold the reigns of your Purpose, Dreams, and the abundance that is waiting to pour into your life. What is the mindset that will manifest your Dream and how will you direct it?

CHAPTER FOUR

What Can I Get You, Ma'am?

"In the long run, we shape our lives, and we shape ourselves. The process never ends until we die. And the choices we make are ultimately our own responsibility."

– ELEANOR ROOSEVELT

I see the Master Order Taker standing behind a big counter ready to serve. There you are with crossed arms, head in the clouds, not paying attention at all. You are clueless as to what you want or even how to read the menu. You feel rushed by life, by others waiting for your decision, by the endless ticking of the clock. Going with the feeling of frustration, you exit the line, allowing others to pass. You are hungry, lost, and unable to recognize the difference between what satisfies and what does not. (If only we could leave the line at fast food restaurants in the same hasty way . . . we'd all be a lot thinner and healthier.)

Before you give up on ordering up your "yellow brick road" with all the fixin's, let's talk about a few basics. You have prioritized your list and decided how much satisfaction you receive from each one. Though you may have placed your Finances in the numeral uno spot, we are going to first address your State of Mind, as I mentioned at the end of the previous chapter. What have you rated this area of your life? Is it a four, a one, perhaps? Wherever it is, I assure you it can, and will, improve with some attention.

Now it's time to look at the distance between the number you chose and the one that you intend to reach. Ask yourself this question: *What would bring your State of Mind to a ten?* I cannot stress enough how important this step is to your success. Your best friend, as wonderful as her advice is, can't help you. This is one quiz you can't cheat on. It needs to come totally from within *you*. Take your time to think, pray, meditate . . . whatever you need to do to feel at peace with your choices. You can always change your mind later! So, relax and have fun.

Think in generalities for this section of the exercise. Let's look at a make believe example I've created from the above list. You currently rate your State of Mind a four, but you desire it to be a ten . . . don't we all. While thinking about how to get it there, you might be tempted to write down the following things:

My State of Mind would be a ten if everyone would . . .

. . . only get a clue.

. . . stop being so lame.

. . . stop blaming me for everything.

. . . stop hurting me.

Notice one thing these statements have in common: They all have to do with others and are negative in connotation. I gave these examples to show you what *NOT* to do. The thing you need to focus on to bridge this satisfaction gap has nothing to do with anyone but you, even if it ultimately affects others. Now, let's look at some more serving examples.

My State of Mind would be a ten . . .

. . . with better communication.

. . . with forgiveness.

. . . with positive influences.

. . . with deeper intimacy with friends and family.

. . . with acceptance of who I am.

Do you see and feel the difference? They generate emotions that serve you just by reading them, unlike the accusatory statements that instantly bring about frustration and anger, ultimately just more destruction. Patterns of negative thinking will keep you below a five on that life scale. Again, I have personal experience to back it up. I first had to deal with my own issues, my doubts and fears, the reasons I had stinkin' thinkin' before putting demands on anyone else. I had to change. News flash: I am still changing!

Okay, so let's see where you are now. You've located yourself in the State of Mind area. You've decided how much you like, or dislike, it there. You know where you see yourself. With a little mental agility you can decide what would add points to your satisfaction level. After doing so, our example statement now looks like this:

> ***My State of Mind is currently a four. It would be a ten with acceptance of who I am.***

You have accomplished more than you think by getting to this point. In fact, you may have just saved your future, including your marriage, job, finances, or all ten areas from untimely death. It's amazing how much revelation comes with small steps. Now, you only need to consider your own situation and create statements with your goals and specific action steps. This is, if nothing else, an exercise that will open up the door to your thought life that is either creating peace and happiness or strife and despair. Let's find out which . . .

CHAPTER FIVE

The Real Work Begins

"Don't limit yourself. Many people limit themselves to what they think they can do. You can go as far as your mind lets you. What you believe, remember, you can achieve."

– MARY KAY ASH

I have every intention of helping you realize there are no limitations on this quest, that you can obtain that elusive "10" in all areas of your life, that you can discover your Purpose and live it. The exercises in this book will help you do just that. They are guiding tools, compasses to keep you on track. You want change? Well, change wants you, too. I have another bold in-your-face nugget for you. I've seen people cry over this next statement, heard them curse, and watched them stand in utter disbelief. Here it goes. Try not to hate me too much.

"Everything you are, everything you have, or don't have, and every problem and victory is a direct result of what you've thought, said, and believed up to this point."

I can hear you thinking . . . excuses. No more of that. Stay with me while I show you—beyond a shadow of doubt—the truth of my words. Don't worry, we'll get back to the exercise in a minute. This is a prerequisite course called the ***clean-up***. You're about to remove some chains, not the pretty, sterling silver kind but the binding, hold-you-back type. And, it has to do with your thoughts and actions that follow. Do you remember "with every action there is a reaction?" Of course, you do. You believe it, right? If you don't, I highly suggest that you observe any boxing match or auto race, eat a super-hot burrito, or create a web site that details all the reasons you hate the president or a particular religion. I'm willing to bet there is a distinct ***REACTION***, all because of the initial action.

Sure, most of my examples could be considered negative, but even if you have good intentions, act out of love, sincerely believe in your effort, doing non-serving things still brings non-serving results. This is especially true for you habitual offenders out there who need to be put away for your chronic insanity. Just kidding. But, you do need to stop expecting to get a different result from the same thought patterns, actions, and core beliefs. Seriously, you are not going to get an apple tree no matter how many times you plant a pear seed in the ground.

I've said all of that to say this: Even when you discover your Purpose, or even if you already know it, failure is almost a sure thing if you have sabotaging thoughts and actually follow through with those non-serving ideas. You must think carefully about the next step.

The Butterfly Payoff

Your success depends on it. Any unwillingness to correct errors, poor behavior, and self-destructive thoughts will keep you planted right where you are. You can read a thousand of these self-development books, but without the right mindset and the proper action, the **Payoff stays merely a seed and does not come to full fruition**.

Do you think you are ready to move on now? If not, it's okay. Stay here until you are. Patience will serve you while you find courage to move forward. But if you are ready, hang on to your hat, 'cause we're goin' for a ride! We've set the stage for major change by making a statement that includes the what (State of Mind) and who (You). It's time to add the why, how, and when. Let's recall the statement, as well as expand it a little for clarity. Remember, I've used the State of Mind not only because it's one of the most important parts of executing life change but as an example of the Rating System that you can apply to all ten life areas.

> **Because my State of Mind (*what*) is important for my life purpose (*why and who*), I want it to be a ten (*what*). I believe it would be a ten if I accepted who I am (what).**

Now, you have several questions to answer for this next part. As I said, we will add the how and when to our statement. I've listed a few things that you could do in this hypothetical situation to find self-acceptance.

- Use positive affirmations

- Counteract negative thoughts with positive ones immediately

- Set aside time for myself

- Engage in an activity I enjoy

- Focus on things I'm passionate about

Though I have listed several suggestions, only one *action* should be focused on at a time to ensure your goal manifests naturally and without the "burn out" I mentioned earlier. There's also that *thing* that happens when you give someone a list of things to do: Rebellion. That's all I'm going to say about that. Just keeping it real, my friend. Okay, now let's choose one of the above actions to apply to our statement. How about using positive affirmations daily? We have the how, what about the when? To keep this subtle and doable, I'm going to say you can do this action once daily. The statement now looks like this:

Because my State of Mind (*what*) is important for my life purpose (*why and who*), I (*who*) want it to be a ten (*what*). I (*who*) believe it would be a ten if I accepted who I am. I can improve my State of Mind by using positive affirmations once a day (how and when).

That wasn't so hard, was it? I didn't think so. There are your thoughts again. What if my State of Mind is poor because of the actions of another? What if I can't do it? What if my brain is too far gone to restore? Despite the fact I'm an optimist at heart, I do believe there are some situations you shouldn't even try to improve or change on your own. Let me explain before you condemn this baby to the drain. There are those of you who may need more specialized help, such as that obtained from a professional therapist or psychologist. Mental illness should not be taken lightly. If you believe your mental state is beyond your means to improve, please seek a doctor before anything else. I mean it!

Something else to consider: Sometimes the kind of change you need challenges your desire to stay in a comfort zone, like with a marriage, a job, a friendship, an addiction, etc. This is the place where it is necessary to understand the significance of making serving choices and acting on them, ridding yourself of dysfunctional thoughts and situations.

To answer the first question: *What if my State of Mind is poor because of the actions of another?* It gets a little complicated here, but it's not the place to start thinking in terms of the impossible. On the contrary, I am feeding you a meal of nothing less than infinite possibilities. Not only will you learn how to overcome an obstacle such as uncooperative people but will gain a skill that lifts you to new heights in every area of your life. It's more about *how* you react to others and situations than what non-serving events are happening *to* you.

Mindset and Trapped Emotions

Throughout our lives we experience a broad range of

emotions that are a normal part of life. Some of them, however, can be extreme enough to become trapped in our bodies, leaving us to filter life and love through them. One of the services I provide for my clients is the release of such trapped emotions. I do this because it generally accelerates any other coaching work we do together. It helps to change the mindset from a deeper place that may be otherwise unreachable by standard means. So far, I've not met anyone who does not have trapped emotions. Renowned holistic physician and lecturer, Dr. Bradley Nelson, introduced the concept in his book, *The Emotion Code*. He believes that these embedded emotions can disrupt our lives in many ways. Ill health, financial issues, relationship problems, and even mental disorders are all possible consequences from allowing them to remain in the body for long periods of time.

Discovering trapped emotions is done with a method called muscle testing that aids in communication with our bodies and subconscious minds. The practitioner asks the client questions (directing them to his or her subconscious) and gets answers with one of several muscle testing methods. These answers come when the body and mind are willing to share this information and when they are ready to release a particular emotion. Once the trapped emotion is identified, the practitioner passes a magnet over the client's main energy meridian that runs down the center of the body. The client's subconscious then indicates, through the same muscle testing method, whether the emotion has truly been released.

With some practice, anyone can release trapped emotions for themselves, as well. Though, I recommend using a practitioner for the first time, you can learn the techniques from Dr. Nelson's book. Whether you work with someone or do it yourself, it is a magnificent compliment to your self-development Journey that I endorse with my whole heart and professional reputation.

Tools like *The Emotion Code* give you an arsenal at your disposal to change your life on a deeper level. Whenever we search within, we find answers that offer significant promise that we will never slip back into to old ways of thinking again. I, myself, have discovered an amazing place of growth and change after experiencing the removal of trapped emotions. Instead of wondering if you can stay on the road to your Dreams, you no longer worry about it. You wake up and spend your days alive and free from that which hindered your Journey in the past. You can't help but cultivate a fresh perspective—a new mindset that paves the way for anything and everything.

CHAPTER SIX

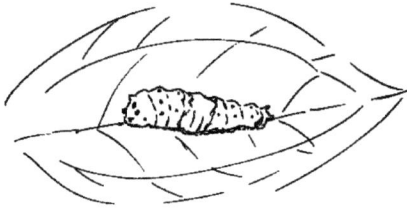

Bring In The Big Guns

"If you keep sincerely asking for what's best, God will give you a very good chance to achieve it - even if you don't believe in God!"

– BILL BLACKMAN

No matter how powerless you have felt in the past or even right now, you need to know there is an endless source of energy available to you . . . more of that arsenal I spoke of earlier. The key is connecting with it and doing so on a regular basis. The source I'm talking about is Divine. It's Spirit, Source, God, Christ, Holy Spirit, the Angels, Chi, the Universe, Masters, Guides, Teachers, and all that is (sorry if I left your deity out of this list). The name you give this source doesn't matter as much as whether you connect to it or not. After that, the details of *your* truth will come. I'm not talking about religion, going to church, or believing in any certain set of rules or doctrine. Simply stated: you are not alone on your Journey.

I've put this spiritual sidetrack here so you don't go off and do all this changing unprepared. That would be like leaving one third of your equipment behind, literally. With the remarkable and delicate three-part structure of our being (body, mind, and spirit), comes a responsibility to balance, nourish, and respect it. You accomplish this through awareness and understanding (*more on that later in the book*). For now, we'll just touch on the spiritual side of things, giving a feel for how an amazing tool called creation (manifestation) really works.

Recall, for a moment, the statement we created as an example of how to improve the State of Mind.

> *"Because my State of Mind is important for my life purpose, I want it to be a ten. I believe it would be a ten if I accepted who I am. I can improve my State of Mind by using positive affirmations once a day."*

Know that in all transition, willingness to work in whatever capacity you can to help things along is valiant, but you also need to let go of or accept what you can't change. By doing so, you are able to enlist Divine Source to take care of that which presents as impossible for you. If you believe your troubles are based on someone else's mistakes or if negative self-doubt fills your mind, you won't grow your State of Mind to a ten. But what you can do is bring your desires to a place within your body, mind, and spirit where they can be nourished with hope, positive emotion, details, and spiritual energy. You have all that you need to do this already. We were created to desire beauty, joy, abundance, and health. It's in our nature.

I won't blow smoke here. Enlisting your spirit, energy, and all that is into your beautiful plan to embrace your highest self requires practice and perseverance. Some people believe that spiritual matters just sort of happen without our consent or intention. I believe we have power to call upon Source energy and to direct it by our intentions. That said, here are two extremely effective meditations for doing just that.

Visualization/Manifestation Exercise

In order to manifest a desire, you first have to bring your mind to calm clarity. Doing this enables you to visualize more effectively. There are many relaxation techniques out there. Meditation, prayer, yoga, deep breathing, listening to music are all wonderful ways to promote well-being. I want you to choose one or two that bring comfort and put you at peace. Again, I'm not here to tell you how to connect to your higher power. If you need to stay within a certain realm of spiritual practice, please do so. The following con-nection meditation has no religious significance. It's just a tool to facilitate the movement of energy through your body.

Three-Point with Gratitude Clearing

Move into a comfortable position and close your eyes. Breathe deeply, relaxing your body. You may want to visualize a warm light entering through your feet. Simply allow it to flow upward until it has encom-passed your entire body, focusing especially on tense areas like your shoulders, neck, and face. This exercise involves four primary areas of your body, the area between your eyebrows, the top of your head, the center of your chest (your heart), and your tailbone area. These specific areas are four of the seven sacred energy portals (Chakras) located throughout your body. It is believed that each of these portals swirl with the very life energy that keeps us whole and healthy and connects us to all life. Focusing on the top of your head, or your crown chakra, enhances your ability to receive from the spiritual realm and the universe. The center of your forehead, just between your eyes, is your third eye chakra. This portal's job is to increase your awareness and intuition, making it easier for you to clearly see that which is spiritual or psychic in nature. And the third area you will focus on for this exercise is your root chakra, located near the perineum between the anus and genitals. This area represents your security, survival, and your future potential. Finally, you will create a deep connection to your heart chakra with a form of gratitude.

(Read through these steps first before attempting the exercise for the first time.)

Focus your attention between your eyes. I've found it extremely helpful to roll my eyes slightly upward for this part. Now, visualize a large, white cloud out in front of you. From that cloud, see a beautiful golden cord floating toward you. See it enter your body through a portal that sits right between your eyebrows. As it does, it is rotating slightly to clear this area of debris and any negative energy. Now, with gentle purpose, allow it to go up through the top of your head. Again, see it rotating in this area. It clears this portal, freeing it to receive all that is waiting to enter your life. Allow this gateway to get as large as it can. The more open it is, the more you will receive. See the cord come back through your crown and proceed down the back of your neck. Feel it pass each vertebra until it rests at your tailbone.

You have worked the golden cord through the first point between your eyes to your crown (the second point), and then to your root (the third point). To complete the triangle, bring it back out the first point but, before you do, send it through your heart, giving it all of your love and gratitude in whatever form serves you. Watch the cord go out and disappear back into the cloud. You may bring the cord back through the course as many times as you like until you feel clear and energized. This clearing exercise prepares you to visualize that which you want to manifest or bring forth into your life.

Three Point Attraction/Manifestation Meditations

When you complete the clearing exercise, remain in the peaceful, relaxed state for the next part. It is now time for you to implement your desires into an effective meditation that expedites the manifestation of what you want. Because you are first addressing your state of mind, you should be targeting that which affects this part of your life. Now visualize the specific thing you want to manifest. If you recall the example: *The woman wants to improve her State of Mind by using positive affirmations daily.* Of course, you should insert your personal goal and vision in place of my example.

Focus on the area between your eyes, as you did with the golden cord. Imagine what your specific "desire" looks like. How does it make you feel in your body? How will this event change your life? See yourself experiencing it now. Hear yourself tell someone about how it has changed your life. Make this image as real as you can. See, feel, touch, taste, and smell the scene. Your mind makes it real. Place your scene into a sphere or bubble. It makes it easier to move it through the body.

When you have clearly filled your mind with this powerful vision and can feel emotion rising, move the sphere to your crown. Let it rest in the portal the cord created. This is where your desire (your vision) will be charged and blessed by Divine Source/God. See the sphere charged with great energy. I visualize electricity inside my sphere, but you can use whatever power source resonates with you. Load your vision to capacity with this powerful force. Allow this to build excitement about having your vision, as though it is being handed to you on a silver platter by the Universe. If you don't feel strong emotion here, keep working on the vision until it connects with you on a deep level.

Your sphere can now move down through the crown and begin its journey down the back of your neck. Continue to feel strong emotions as related to your desire. It's normal to have sensations of warmth, tingling, or nothing at all, as it travels down your spine. Simply allow it to move freely. Stop the vision at your root for just a moment. This is the actualization of your desire, the representation of your vision grounding into your experience. You've accepted it. As you did with the cord, bring your sphere to your heart. Hold it there. Thank God and all Divine Source for giving you this vision and for manifesting it into your reality. All expressions of love and gratitude are appropriate here, but I pretend that I'm thanking someone who just gifted me my most elaborate Dream, even if it's just a simple thing. When you are ready, complete the exercise by moving the vision through the portal between your eyes. Watch it float away from your body, into the white cloud. Sometimes I visualize my sphere breaking up into thousands of colored light beams that dive to the earth, where they will execute all that needs to happen to make my vision a reality. Repeat this exercise twice more.

After you've completed your first experience with this meditation, pay attention to how your body feels. Most people feel a little light-headed or airy immediately following the exercise, kind of like after a massage or spa treatment. Give yourself time to recover fully before you move or start other activities.

This is also a good time to journal what you envisioned, so you can refer to it later when it comes to pass. Engage in this exercise as much as you can until your desire/need manifests. Remember, with something as effective as this, you may begin to see results almost immediately. Notice your attitude changing first. It's difficult to be frustrated, angry, and doubtful when you *believe* your Dreams are coming true. Manifestation is nothing more than believing in something so much that it overwhelms you with gratitude and joy before it physically appears in this world. Call it faith, if you like. That's the only *secret* you need to know.

Your Belief System

"Faith consists in believing when it is beyond the power of reason to believe. It is not enough that a thing be possible for it to be believed."

– VOLTAIRE

This world is full of chronic doubters—those who can't possibly believe in something until it smacks them in the face . . . a shame really, considering what joy rests in a little faith. This is one of the topics to which you should pay close attention. This next sentence will change your life.

You will never manifest anything outside of what you believe.

Don't be fooled into thinking that everything you've always wanted will just show up on your doorstep one day without you believing it can happen. That kind of faith doesn't just happen overnight. Well, in most cases it doesn't. How is it that some people seem to get all of their Dreams manifested in a relatively short period of time? Part of the answer may be that they were trained as children or teens to believe in evolving as people and bettering their spiritual lives. They learned to acknowledge (show gratitude) for success and happiness at that level. The longer you believe in infinite possibilities, the faster the seemingly imposs-ible happens.

Believing in something is an "**action**" that causes a "**reaction.**" There is a distinct energy involved in this process:

    desire→

        emotional response→

           belief →

                greater emotional response→

                greater belief→

                  manifestation

Let's break that down: You desire a thing, an event, or perhaps an opportunity, you want it so badly, you feel it actually attach to your body and mind. Because of your emotional drive, you begin to focus on it with passion, believing that it's going to happen. The more you Dream about and visualize your desires, the more you believe and impart emotion into your vision. It's like building a tower to reach the clouds—your Dream clouds. The wonderful thing is your "Dream Clouds" meet you half way. They travel closer every day—a mutual attraction that ends in the fulfillment of your vision.

This process not only manifests "things," but it changes you from the inside out. Your attitude changes and so does your mind. Suddenly, you believe in the manifestation of your Dreams not only for your benefit but for the greater good of mankind. And when you see how the concept works for smaller Dreams, you begin to believe in larger wonders that change the world. You may even realize that some of those "things" you thought you wanted aren't so important anymore. It's funny how self-development promotes new ideas and Dreams. It's a fair assumption that this ability wasn't gifted to us to only manifest fancy sports cars all day long. Though, there is nothing wrong with having nice things, but the "greater good" involves so much more. But, hey, serving mankind from a little red convertible is something this messenger approves of 100%!

Think about what happens when you do a charity drive to benefit a great cause: People show up with their time, money, and gifts. Now, if you were to do that same drive to benefit just yourself, I'm betting you would not see the same response and results. Well, what if the Universe sees it that way, too? What if we get more Divine excitement and help for our Dreams when they involve "a great cause?" Just something to think about when you develop your vision for the future based on your Purpose.

CHAPTER SEVEN

Purpose: Better Than Chocolate

"Our deepest fear is not that we are inadequate. Our deepest fear is that we are powerful beyond measure. It is our light not our darkness that frightens us. We ask ourselves, who am I to be brilliant, gorgeous, talented, fabulous? Actually, who are you not to be? You are a child of God. Your playing small doesn't serve the world. There's nothing enlightened about shrinking so that other people won't feel insecure around you. We were born to make manifest the glory of God that is within us."
– NELSON MANDELA, INAUGURAL ADDRESS
– WRITTEN BY MARIANNE WILLIAMSON

I speculate that the question "Why am I here?" is asked (at least thought) more frequently than any other cosmic inquiry. The quest for Purpose has driven the human soul for thousands of years. Without it, most find little consolation in the trivial distractions offered by the world . . . unless you consider chocolate, that is. I compared the two in the chapter title just for you. I know it takes a lot for most women to give up their favorite chocolate treat, especially during that "special" time of the month. Knowing your Purpose is more satisfying than the finest chocolate ever made . . . really, it's that good. I don't say that precariously. Proving it is *my* Purpose.

I realized every morning only one thing stirred my heart, something for which I had passion. It was time to pay attention to the message that said:

You will help others discover their Purpose and fulfill it.

Of course, other indications and confirmations popped up over the course of my life, but the season to fully manifest it had arrived. (Here's the part where I tell you about my enlightenment.) Opportunities arrived that I could not have found if I had looked for them. People, mentors, teachers, friends, and clients came out of nowhere to meet me on my Journey. My Dreams were coming to pass (still are and will continue to do so).

As rare as it is for me to have no words, I find it difficult to describe the overwhelming gratitude and joy I feel knowing why I'm here and that I'm acting on that Purpose daily. I never really understood what true joy meant until I accepted my calling and moved into it. The things I used to deem important aren't so much anymore. What changed? My perspective. It was like finding my soul mate or a single red rose amidst a thousand white. Our gifts and callings are manifested from the light of Divine Love and God's presence. The brightness is overwhelming at times but beautiful and irresistible. You don't want to look away, knowing the Journey will not be as delicious without understanding your ultimate Purpose.

The key: move with joy and Purpose . . . and, always bring the chocolate.

I mentioned earlier in this section about writing a novel. Well, here's the rest of that story:

While forced to spend most of my time in bed with the devastating migraine pain, I had a thought that changed my life: *What if this unfortunate event has a Purpose? What if there is a reason I'm in this place?* You can see I desperately wanted to make something positive out of a pitiful situation. The brainstorm eventually led me to start a novel that had a character who suffered from migraine headaches. However, *her* pain had an interesting Purpose.

I won't outline my first fiction work here, but I will tell you that it changed my life. Why? Because my endeavors reminded me of a deep-set gift I'd let slip into the filing cabinet of life: writing. I started thinking about how seemingly negative circumstances—a series of unfortunate events—can be a catalyst for unprecedented life-change. Writing the book was also extremely therapeutic. I released a deep down part of myself—a part I had buried for many years. Even though I still had headaches that challenged my everyday life, I moved on toward my Purpose and

Dreams and haven't stopped since. You can execute your Dreams during difficult times, and you can glean invaluable resources and wisdom with which to help others.

How to Recognize What Is in Front of You

The reason so many women struggle to define Purpose is they can't see what is too close to them. Now, if you're delightfully past your thirties, then you understand what can happen to your eyesight in a short period of time. But for you younger gals, I'll explain: Sometime between 2:00 AM and 6:00 AM (give or take a few hours) on your fortieth birthday, your eyes decide they no longer want to focus on anything closer than two feet away. It was a sad day when I needed reading glasses to see the face of my newborn daughter that I gave birth to at age forty-one. My point: When things are too close or too simple, sometimes we can't or won't focus on them. We want drama and complication—a puzzle to solve. The obvious becomes a shade of gray while we search for clarity elsewhere.

Look, you've been doing this avoiding-the-obvious dance in some form your whole life. If not, you've at least thought about it. Really. It's that simple. My life has always been filled with family and a large number of creative ventures—mainstays I have, on occasion, taken for granted. The other thing that kept tapping me on the shoulder was the helping others thing. I often found myself looking for opportunities to give life direction, healing, or simple encouragement. I did apply many of my skills and interests over the years, but I still needed clarity about my authentic self.

I'd like to share with you the moment I saw things clearly, as quoted from an article I posted on my global women's community website, Womenslifelink.com.

Defining Purpose in 60-Minutes or Less

I did an exercise this week for a course I'm taking. It entailed writing down all of my natural skills, learned skills, things I've overcome, and all of my experiences. When I was finished, the paper in front of me looked like it had been written during a first-time Spirograph session. I could hardly read the hodge-podge of words that I precariously penned. Because the events of my life weren't spilling out in order, I found the chaos mimicked my sporadic memories. I do have a point telling you about my sloppy assignment.

As I stared at the red chicken scratch, I suddenly realized that our lives produce millions of thoughts, events, experiences, skills, and traumas that stay dormant in our minds or forgotten altogether. We even dismiss these shards of our lives as insignificant when, truthfully, even the little things are important. The question posted in my mind: Could this mixed up thought pattern be the reason why people have trouble discovering their purpose? I heard an unequivocal, "YES!"

After organizing what I'd written into categories, I was amazed at the clarity that came to me. Though I've known the basic outline of my life-calling, the specifics and transparency of it had not been revealed until that moment. The next step of the exercise waved the magic wand that brought it all together. I was asked to finish this sentence:

To me, the perfect world looks like . . .

I finished it with a description of a butterfly flying freely. She is exactly what she's supposed to be, nothing more and nothing less. Knowing this makes her live it every moment of her life. Additionally, I saw a cascading waterfall that nourished every living thing around it with a powerful flow of energy and life.

My mentor/coach said, "Kellie, that is your Purpose." I knew she was right. It melted into my spirit like sweet, undefiled honey. I was overcome with joy and gratitude. I am here to help others find their Purpose and ability to be themselves by encouraging and refreshing them. Of course, there are many details that go with that synopsis, but the simple statement is profound to me.

———————————————

There is no need to travel half way around the world, take multiple personality profiles, or ask your friends to tell you what they think you should be doing. Just look in your home, within your own heart, in the eyes of your children, at the passions you hold nearest and dearest . . . remember Dorothy's journey into chaos only to discover that her heart was in her own backyard. If you still don't get anything after that, please call me for an appointment. We need to talk.

CHAPTER EIGHT

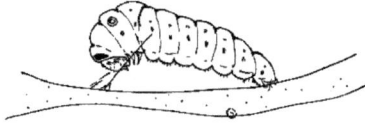

Listening To Your Authentic Self

"Let your heart guide you. It whispers softly, so listen closely."

– ANONYMOUS

Pressure, trauma, drastic change, and crisis situations are all events that stress the very core of who we are. But guess what? Our fabulously designed beings can handle most anything, if we listen to the messages (the loud and subtle ones), releasing the reigns long enough to allow autonomic healing. If you are anything like me, you like to be in control of what happens around you. It's difficult to let things *just be* at times, to listen to that still small voice, to live each moment with the clarity that it is-what it is.

One blatant culprit for our incessant need to fix everything is our current culture. Society pressures us to fit into molds that shouldn't exist in the first place. We only think we are wrong or something *is* wrong with us because someone else told us so. This is the place (the stuffy box) where syndromes and conditions are born. Relax. You are exactly who you are meant to be. The drive to be a happier, well-rounded person should come from deep passions and pursuit of

Purpose, not from unrealistic societal ideals.

Your truth comes as you experience these difficulties, however. Understanding that we cannot be all things to all people by serving their every whim is the perfect lesson in the flawless classroom of life. That's why it doesn't matter where you are on this Journey or how far away from truth you feel you are. Your starting point is always right now in this moment. Discovery and lessons bloom in every situation and challenge. You need only to listen with your whole being and pay attention to your reactions.

The Night Messenger: Are You Listening?

You wake up in a sweat, terrified by the images from a reoccurring nightmare. The question "What the hell does that mean?" haunts you until eventually the dream and details slip through the crevices of your subconscious mind. I've lived this scenario far too many times to count and definitely too many to talk about here. The interesting thing about dreams and our psyche is there are no flukes or mistakes. Our minds process that which needs to come to the forefront one way or another. Often we ignore conscious signs of this process, so the subconscious has no choice but to take over the project . . . so to speak.

I'm not saying every dream has a deep spiritual, life-changing meaning, but reoccurring symbols, people, objects, and places could be messages worth paying attention to. The reason I'm even talking about this is to help you understand that your human experience, your entire life is a well-oiled machine that moves from one second to the next with drive and Purpose even if you're not aware of it. That's why it's important to listen to your inner voice, to your dreams, to every pivotal idea. I've discovered so much about myself through this type of self-communication and listening.

Though dreams can be a powerful way to recognize inner stress and cumulative issues, the body has other significant ways to speak to us; such as, physical pain and conditions, tears, joy, intuitive knowledge, sense of wellbeing or the opposite sense that something is wrong. How often have you ignored the above signs of communication from your authentic self? Don't worry, we all miss them and even purposely dismiss them on occasion, depending on the message. We don't do something or stop doing it unless there is a Payoff. Ignoring the soul's cry for help may be a coping mechanism to detour severe pain or fear. Unfortunately, this practice usually only prolongs stress and prevents true change and personal growth.

Stuck in a Vice

Let's face it, how often do we turn to medications and vices (alcohol, cigarettes, drugs, shopping, gambling, caffeine, food, sugar, or sex) to calm the raging storm we call life? Though all of these forms of temporary relief may receive negative connotations, you have to understand the process on a much deeper level—the level of your authentic self where a positive component of your growth may be in action.

If you have ever found or currently find yourself in the grips of an addiction or self-soothing habit, understand that there is something you need, otherwise, you wouldn't be doing it—the Payoff. The key is to discover the root cause of the distraction by listening to the deepest, purest part of your being. This is where your authentic self resides. We all have a built-in desire to succeed, to be happy, to make others proud, and to fulfill our potential. The answers are in this natural drive. While some find this process easy—getting it right the first time—the majority don't and need rest stops and redos along the way. These breaks from life surface (more like sneak up) in the form of coping mechanisms that aren't always healthful or even logical.

I'm not condoning self-destructive habits or detrimental practices, but I do know this: Beating yourself up for behavior that doesn't reflect your authentic self does *NOT* help the situation! The more negative vibrations and emotions you send out into the universe, the more they come back to you. Instead, listen to what your heart says, to what it needs in order to resolve past issues and dysfunction. Yes, I know this is easier said than done, but judging yourself brings more pain and more need for escape and the vice itself.

I wish I had all of the answers, but I don't. Each woman is different, with varying needs and desires. There is no formula or self-help book to miraculously make everything perfect. It's a process that each one of us has to go through at our own pace, with our own methods of clarification and resolve. Be at peace with yourself and where you are today. Change and growth come faster with that amity. Allow yourself time to work through personal challenges, just as you would patiently comfort and support your best friend if the issues belonged to her or him. Be your own best friend.

Listening to your authentic self requires patience, perseverance, and emotions that demand to be felt. And, just when you think you've got it all figured out, something else comes to the surface to be acknowledged. This is that fork-in-the-road place where you must decide whether to hold on tight or gracefully let go of that which is pushing its way onto your path. Learning constructive ways to cope with challenge will always serve to prove how flexible you are and how beneficial it is to listen to what your authentic self communicates. When it feels good to your soul, to your body, to your spirit, it's authentic.

CHAPTER NINE

Expanding Your Authentic Self

"The world we see that seems so insane is the result of a belief system that is not working. To perceive the world differently, we must be willing to change our belief system, let the past slip away, expand our sense of now, and dissolve the fear in our minds."

– WILLIAM JAMES

I'm sure most of you would agree that we do a fairly good job of expanding our waistlines. Unfortunately, that's not the kind of expansion we need. Once you get in touch with who you are deep down, it's a little easier to feed your authentic self . . . as easy as pie (sorry, couldn't resist that one). One of the main problems we face as women is we tend to "feed" the wrong parts of ourselves, thinking that the process will help us become someone new, someone different, when, truly, all we need to do is just be who we already are.

In the last chapter I talked about listening to your authentic self. This is so important if you want to recognize her, build a relationship with her, and bring her to the forefront of your existence. The genuine *you* might be a little shy, that's where coaxing and cooing comes in. You draw her out by offering her a reward. Here's that word again . . . Payoff. Give her your full attention and find out what it is she really wants, what makes it worth her while to come out and play. My authentic self gets excited about helping others and being heard. When I give her the opportunity to do those things, she responds graciously. And the more she comes out, the more she is expanded and fulfilled. I guarantee yours will do the same.

I love how Goddess Lifestyle Plan's creatrix, Lisa Marie Rosati, explains what being authentic means: *"An authentic woman is a woman who is 100% herself. Authenticity only comes when you are willing to fully self-examine who you are . . . to be SUPER CLEAR about who you are—including the parts of you that you don't particularly like. So, an authentic woman gets who she is—warts and all—and also understands her personal expression—you know, the way she holds space in the world. I think that the authentic woman is not afraid to be completely true to herself. I can tell you from personal experience that authenticity does not come with people pleasing. An authentic woman is strong in her personal convictions and integrity, knows herself inside and out, and loves herself completely—both her shadows and her light."*

I get goose bumps when I read about the feminine shift that brings our truth and all of our beauty to the table. We don't have to hide our insecurities and weaknesses anymore because they are a part of us. And if some people decide after we reveal ourselves that they don't like us or that we are not valuable enough to be in their lives, then so what! We've lost nothing but baggage that holds us back. Let no one decide for you who you should be or how you should act. It's our choice what we want to change and what we want to leave alone. Stick around, you'll get to read more of Lisa Marie's amazing perspective in her story later in the book.

Making Decisions

There is another thing that seems to come up frequently when in pursuit of Purpose and authentic personality: the desire to make life-serving decisions. Decision-making isn't really rocket science. Well, I guess it is if you are a rocket scientist. But, I think it's safe to assume that most of you reading this are not. I learned a little trick somewhere on my own Journey that takes the guesswork out of even the tough decisions. If you feel expanded by a decision, it's likely your authentic self raising the roof. On the other hand, if you feel confused and indifferent about a choice, it's that same gal vibrating at a much lower level, trying to tell you to either wait, to change something or axe the idea completely. Are you getting this? Plain and simple: If it doesn't feel right, don't do it or at least give yourself some time to explore it further. Senses and emotions are tools you want to learn how to use.

As you cozy up to your authentic self, you simultaneously cultivate your intuitive abilities, which also help you to recognize and embrace truth about yourself. That hidden gem of a gal you once thought impossible to understand opens up like a best pal you haven't seen for a month. This is your opportunity to listen with everything you've got. Also, be prepared to not always like what you feel or hear. We all have shadows attached to our lives—many, we may have tried to hide for most of our existence. Truth takes time, and it certainly isn't always pleasant. Expanding the authentic is embracing all of who we are, not just the pretty, sparkly parts. The balance of both sides is what keeps the world turning and makes seeking and experience the grandest version of ourselves possible. Finding this balance requires rehearsal and the willingness to say "yes" to ourselves.

Don't Take "NO" for an Answer

Do you go through emotional cycles that take you from elation to the depths of despair in short periods of time? Do you wonder why you can't seem to keep things even-keeled and running smoothly? Do you wish you weren't constantly moved by your circumstances whether good or bad? Well, I can say that I've experienced all of the above . . . even some recently. Most of this way of thinking comes from the core beliefs we have about ourselves, our place in the world, and our relationship to others. It's likely that true self was denied during these times. What we see and think we know about who we are can provoke the scariest roller coaster ride ever—one that ending is not easy but doable with some training.

Have you ever been to a professional, a doctor or lawyer and asked for advice? I'm sure you have. When we seek out others for answers, we usually accept what we get as the "truth" or at least reasonable and worthy of our time and money. Right? They give the perception of authenticity, so it's easier to trust them. We don't waste any time picking up that prescription or getting that test done. We act immediately on what we *believe* is in our best interest. But for some reason, when it comes to trusting our own intuitions and self-knowing, we cringe or find multiple ways to avoid what we hear, what we know, what we should be acting upon. Well, maybe we don't do this all the time but definitely enough that it keeps us from reaching most of our goals and Dreams. I realized that I tend to say "no" to myself by avoiding the important steps. The "no" is expressed in many different ways. It can be procrastination, avoidance, self-sabotage, anger, illness, depression, and my favorite: excuses! Hitting home again?

So now the only thing to do is stop saying "no" to yourself and start saying, "YES!" This is a true grit moment. It's the nose-to-the-grindstone event that changes everything about your life. It's the decision to make something different happen. It's you and me being who we already are . . . our authentic selves.

The "*YES*" Exercise
(Read through completely before doing the exercise.)

Relax, get really comfortable, and visualize walking down a long corridor with doors along both sides. Now, open each one with the understanding that a different place and opportunity is on the other side.

See and hear yourself talking about these places. Feel yourself enjoying the benefits of your opportunities: money, friends, time, recognition, satisfaction, and whatever else brings you joy and peace. Most importantly, know that you have the right to say "YES" to any of them or all of them! This is a key to changing those misguided core beliefs. We all have places to go and people to meet. We have Purpose and gifts to be utilized. There's only one way to do that: Walk through those doors and just say, "Yes!" This can be a powerful time of connection to your authentic self and your sacred Purpose if you allow yourself to Dream and not second guess what you envision.

Once you choose to walk through a door and set intention to allow that thing or event to happen in your life, you eject a commanding signal to the universe that says you are ready and willing to experience all that it takes to receive it fully. You can also connect this exercise with your manifestation meditation in chapter six to create a stronger emotional response. Don't forget to write down your "yes" choices along with a statement of intention or maybe even a target date by which to accomplish or receive it.

One of the most significant moments of my self-development Journey was when I realized the connection between my Dreams and my Purpose. This understanding is like getting a giant permission slip to do more of what you love and to generate more joy and passion for life. There is no need to search high and low for Purpose because it is likely staring you right in the face in the form of your preferences, passions, personality, and talents. As you look closely at these beautiful characteristics and gifts, consider how you form life Dreams and intend to fulfill them.

PART II

WHAT DREAMS MAY COME?

CHAPTER TEN

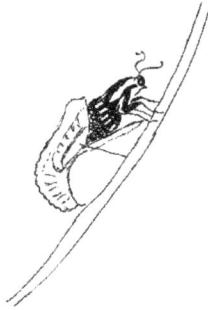

Dream Seed

"Go confidently in the direction of your dreams.
Live the life you have imagined."
— HENRY DAVID THOUREAU

One of the most potent statements I've ever read on life Dreams was in Steve Moore's book, *The Dream Cycle*. He says: *"Lasting personal development must be fueled by a reservoir of inner motivation, an underground river of desire that pumps life and energy to your journey. I believe you will find that source of power in your dreams.*

Of all the possible sources of motivation, none is more powerful than a dream. In the wide-open spaces of your dreams, there are deep wells of motivation that you must tap into and drink from regularly if you are to endure the searing heat of the desert seasons through which your life will certainly pass. During those times, your dreams will sustain you."

In other words, you can't survive without the hope and energy that your Dreams give. I love the example of an "underground river of desire" used in Steve's text. I believe he nailed it with the realization that Dreams are fueled by an unseen force, something we don't just experience without effort. Before modern plumbing graced households all over the world, men (and women) toiled, sometimes days, to dig reliable wells to serve their families. Their greatest hope was that the spot in which they dug was, indeed, in line with some underground water source. Can you imagine working long hours in the hot sun, only to find out your land contained no water? Most of us can't, I'm sure.

I liken this problematic scenario to spending hours, days, weeks, even years working toward a goal without tapping into a sustaining source. You tire, burn out, and decidedly get confused about whether you are digging in the right place. I particularly relate to this, considering I did just that. I toiled to bring meaning to my life without understanding my Purpose or tapping into my Dream source. However, I since have acquired a magic divining rod, of sort—an endless resource of Dream-sustaining energy. I've done so through years of practice and many disappointments, though. I'm willing to bet you've walked on a similar path. Well, it's time for you to drink from your own "underground river." But, first, you must find it. A Dream can be as simple as wanting to bring financial security to your family, or as complicated as feeding a nation of starving children. No matter how small or large your Dream is, I guarantee it's important. And, the Universe will help it come to pass if it's from your authentic self.

Knowing Your Dream Is Authentic

Have goose bumps ever appeared suddenly on your arms when you spoke of something that moved you emotionally? Do you experience ill feelings after making a decision about which you're not sure? Our bodies respond to serving thoughts, energies, and Divine ideas, as well as to those which don't serve. Though you probably should not go and make life-altering decisions based on a couple of goose bumps, I do recommend paying attention to how your body responds physically to those choices. The more you practice feeling into your intuitions, the closer you get to understanding and trusting your subconscious. Chances are, you know the right thing to do in most cases and, for those times when you still are not clear, prayer and meditation often clear up any confusion.

If Dreams are divinely created in us from the beginning, they are there for us to fulfill—a simple concept of direction I live by. Our conscious choice to move those Dreams into reality is the substance that paves the path along the way. This "path" is full of twists and turns, hills and valleys, and sometimes even dangerous obstacles to overcome. Well-thought out plans—those that go through the spiritual test of prayer and deeper conscious contemplation—create a clearer path on which to tread: a Dream bull dozer, if you will. And you better have that "drink" with you at all times. Remember Steve Moore's "desert seasons?"

Have you ever awakened so thirsty your tongue literally stuck to the roof of your mouth? You can't drink that glass of water on your nightstand fast enough. We should think of fulfilling our Dreams like that—a desperate need to move things in the right direction. Now, think about how that refreshing drink satisfies. Fulfilling an authentic Dream from your authentic self feels like that. Amazing. A heart-warming story comes to mind—one that I'm sure will inspire and tickle your soul. Alexa Linton shared her experience with me recently.

Alexa Linton's Story

She didn't look like much of a horse. Brown, with tangled black mane and tail, outgrown hooves, sway back and dirt from head to toe, her overall appearance was, well, lack luster. A girl friend had described her, in her pragmatic way, as behaviorally challenged and, judging from the scrapes and scratches on her herd mates, that wasn't the half of it. Her infamous reputation preceding her, from unwilling and volatile pack horse to unpredictable riding horse to the unfortunate accident that left her owner with a leg broken in three places and no room at the inn, Diamond's life was moving rapidly towards an early and abrupt ending. She was, in all eyes, including her own, not worth very much at all.

This, as you might have guessed, is where I come in. Riding a wave of what might have been either inspiration or insanity, or perhaps the perfect mix of both, I had just arrived home from an apprenticeship feeling very much like I could take over the world. When my friend told me

Diamond's sad story, I felt compelled to meet her. After eight years of working with energy medicine and horses as an Equine Sport Therapist, I figured I could, at the very least, get a read on her and be a bit of help and, at the most, well, I hadn't really thought that far ahead yet.

I arrived at the barn and within minutes of meeting this little brown horse had made the impulsive, perhaps even crazy, decision to take her on, feeling certain that it was far too soon for her fiery, albeit controversial, existence to come to an end. As my second horse, the plan was that she would be a companion for my mare Diva, partaking in an Equine Facilitated Learning program that I was deter-mined to create. Unfortunately, given my impulsiveness, a change in plans, and the weighty absence of a plan B, I found myself face-to-face with one of the most angry and wounded horses I had ever met— unridable, unpredictable and most definitely unsellable.

After a few weeks of working with her on the ground, it became abundantly clear how deeply and profoundly upset she was. In a last ditch effort to find some clarity and hopefully some connection, she was soon on the trailer to a dear friend for training. The turning point came about a month in, after several emails from Stef, pronouncing Diamond the dirtiest little horse she'd ever met. She'd even taken to blanketing her to keep her from rolling in her own urine and feces.

She was, in no uncertain terms, a mess and I wondered if she might ever live up to her name, or if, ironically, she already was, showing us the effects of being irreparably hardened by life's blows. I knew, when Stef sent me an email relating a terrible and potentially catastrophic ride with Diamond that there were some crucial choices to be made. That same night I changed her name. The inspiration for her new name came suddenly along with the process of the ritual I performed—a cleansing of the dense and terrible heaviness of her pain-filled past. It was time for her to be born again as Dreamweaver— a rebirth that no doubt changed my own life irrevocably.

The initial change was subtle but magical none-the-less, not only in Dream, but in those around her, a soft-ening and gradual, tentative blossoming. When she arrived home several months later, disregarding any teachings to "get things done," we embarked on six months of doing nothing with the occasional BodyTalk session and massage work-over thrown in with a heavy daily dose of positive reinforcement. In doing nothing, the unraveling occurred naturally, our tough exteriors breaking down slowly— an organic process unfolding without effort or striving.

When, on a sun-filled day, Dreamweaver "asked" to be ridden for the first time, my excitement was palpable along with my grat-itude. Later, when she asked a dear friend to climb aboard while completely bare of equipment, sidling up to the fence to allow her easy access to her back, I cried, so touched by this gesture and the softness that was enveloping all of her now-stunning features. Like a trail of delicious surrender, more events like these would occur one-by-one, symbols of deepening trust and connection, her beauty and presence becoming more pronounced with each one of these precious moments, coat gleaming, back stronger. Like a beacon, she began to attract people to her, and I would find them often hanging on her fence admiring her, sharing a secret or snuggle, finding ways to connect with this little horse.

I like to think that things are related, that journeys parallel. Mine, during this time, was one of such impressive butterfly-like transformation that I can only compare it to the unprecedented change in this little brown horse, who now gleamed like copper and possessed a beauty and fiery spirit that is hard to describe. Dreamweaver, so aptly named, was helping me rework my world while I helped her rework hers. As I moved through the phases of my transformation, she remained a strong and steady companion, launching me into the work as surely as she was there to pull me through to the next phase. Only now looking back, do I grasp the magnitude of what she was able to accomplish—an entire re-build of the framework of not one but two lives. A foundation strong enough to support my biggest, wildest dreams— a knowing of my inherent value no matter what my experiences might tell me otherwise and a deep trust in the possibility of a life greater than imagined.

Dreamweaver has since found her own perfect person, becoming the heart horse to one of my long-time and most favorite clients, her biggest, wildest dream coming to fruition by way of a deep love and connection just for her. She lives in a field next to a river with another horse surrounded by eagle nests and greets each day and her person with cuddles unrivaled. She ventures into my sessions often, teaching of following your heart and never ever giving up on yourself even when it seems all is lost, of mothering your own spirit, being tender and yet daring enough to ask for what may seem impossible. And not surprisingly, her person has found the innate strength and self-worth to ask for her wildest and biggest dreams and I have the distinct pleasure of sitting back and watching them come true one-by-one. She does live with and love a horse called Dreamweaver, after all.

I love that Alexa was able to recognize the Dream seed in Dreamweaver and in herself. So many times the Universe shows us things via mirrors that are all around us, and we just simply don't pay attention. What seeds do you sense are waiting to pop open with life? And, remember, just because it's small right now doesn't mean it isn't a big Dream.

Though we will go over Dreaming big later, I want to touch on it here. I believe Dreams are something that should have no limitations (like the seedling's potential). The images and hopes you have now are meant to be explored and experienced no matter how big or small they seem to you. Even things that don't make sense to you or others are valid and carry Purpose with them. It could be that those fantastic Dreams you have are meant to bring you up to a new place, to a new way of thinking. No matter what their ultimate Purpose is, it's your responsibility to hold onto them with all your might and treat them with respect, as Alexa did with Dreamweaver. No one else will do this for you.

We both know that "obstacles" will show up. It is during those times where your commitment gets challenged. Even as I'm writing this, several road blocks have appeared on my Journey, forcing me to anchor myself further to my Dream and my Purpose. It's hard sometimes but worth every ounce of energy and time spent to procure fulfillment. In all honesty, you possess the power to change your life and to create the environment where Dreams come to pass. You need only believe it.

CHAPTER ELEVEN

Listening To Your Authentic Self

"If you don't like something, change it. If you can't change it, change the way you think about it."
— MARY ENGELBREIT

As women, we naturally guide the heart-center and atmosphere of our homes. We feel more. We believe more, and we certainly create enthusiasm when we need to. And, unfortunately, we can also tear down everything we've worked for with that same power when it's influenced by negative emotions that don't serve us. If you despair over circumstances or a difficult situation to the point of emotional compromise, your family and friends feel it. They go there with you whether you want them to or not.

More so now than ever before, women need to stand up and take control of their emotional behavior and start bringing joy and peace back to the home and world. It starts with you, with me, with us all. I coach women every week and see, first hand, how feelings of

91

defeat and self-doubt can render them helpless. I'm telling you what I tell them: "The buck stops here! Own it." No matter how bad things seem to be, they will change. How they change and how fast are factors up to you. What will you focus on? Will you be brave enough to believe in your Purpose and your Dreams? Will you work on remembering your true self so others can benefit from the manifestation of your Dreams?

There's no greater feeling than knowing *you* affected someone's life because *you* changed something about yourself. This is the kind of power we have. No one blocks us from seeing every desire and Purpose unfold before our eyes. It's all there ready to be gotten, to be picked like a fragrant flower from the meadow, to be pollinated by the feet of a beautiful butterfly. I am amazed, and so very grateful, each time my Dreams show up. They aren't all monumental, but they are important to me. It builds my faith, the tower to my "Dream cloud." Even writing this book was a manifestation of a goal—a vision I had for a long time. We don't always know how long things will take to change or to manifest. Patience and diligence are often tested. With all my heart, I believe this is by design. Truly, if we knew all things in advance, we would not be able to carry the load. We would likely have some sort of emotional breakdown with the weight of seeing the whole picture. Knowledge comes with the acceptance of responsibility and when all three parts of our being are ready for it. When the student is ready, the teacher shows up and the Journey continues.

The Universe and Divinity knows us better than we

presently know ourselves. Any hesitation on that of Divine Source/God to give us information or to manifest something is for a good reason. Understand the big picture is at stake, the "greater good of mankind." The interconnectedness of all things makes for interesting logistics and planning. Don't think I want that job . . . and neither should you. So, next time you want it all and you want it now . . . reconsider your position.

Receiving the Payoff of your life Journey is also about perspective. I remember traveling through the mountains in Pennsylvania while on a family vacation. Though the view was spectacular, I found myself petrified of the curvy, hilly road that did not allow clear sight of what was ahead. My fear stole the joy of being with my family in that wonderful new place. The unknown tainted my perspective. What I should have been doing was enjoying the Journey instead of visualizing the van careening over the edge into the deep valley below. Action and reaction is the key here. By continually moving forward, each step brings understanding along the way. The path is revealed as a result of your natural movement.

It's so crucial to look more closely at who you are before moving in every direction but the right one. All you get from that is dizzy. Trust me, I'm rather motion sensitive in more ways than one. Starting things and choosing not to finish them nauseates and paralyzes. You begin wondering why you try to accomplish anything at all. Sooner than later, you stop trying. But you never have to travel that road again. There, I said it. You can do all things with Purpose by having a different perspective—a little understanding of why you're here brings Dreams to life.

The Dream Thieves

Whether you want to believe it or not, there are some nasty criminals wreaking havoc in the lives of many women. They steal, control, mock, hinder, use, destroy, and even kill in some cases. Though these perpetrators are not physical thugs, they are still dangerous as they can keep beautiful, talented women (like you) captive.

These inner roadblocks are usually made up of a combination of different emotions and beliefs that remain hidden until we wake up and face them: fear of rejection, fear of hurting others, fear of getting attention, fear of being hurt, fear of not being good enough . . . well, just a whole lot of fear that seems to have multiple personality disorder. Below I've highlighted some of the worst criminals, their deviant plans, and how they have been caught. Though I've brought a little humor to this section, please consider its implications with all seriousness.

Call the Paddy Wagon!

1. Wanted: Fear

Fear is a multi-faceted, unpleasant mastermind

criminal who exists by the belief that someone or something is dangerous, likely to cause pain and suffering. Fear also thinks it belongs. It was a necessary component to survival in the ancient days and remains a needed emotion to keep us from jumping off of cliffs and walking down dark, dangerous alleys . . . it should, anyway. However, fear is given WAY too much freedom these days. It has become a ruler in the lives of so many. It makes its victims pass up opportunities and even reject people. Fear needs rehabilitation.

Arrest Report: Today, fear was arrested for violently protesting Dreams and goals. The suspect was apprehended in the mind of a woman who didn't even know it was there. Officers encouraged the victim by teaching that **facing fears would free her**. They also took the vic through several **coaching sessions** to release the fear. The woman is now free to pursue her life Dreams without the intruder getting in the way.

2. Wanted: Limiting Beliefs

These criminals are the thoughts and/or stories you tell yourself that do not support you in living in your Authentic Power. Limiting beliefs impact the choices you make and how you behave in any given situation. This gang is sneaky and hides in the core of its victims. Limiting Beliefs can take over control of almost anyone who refuses to evaluate what he or she truly believes. Its origins and support are linked to family, friends, religion, media, and connections to fear. Be cautious when apprehending Limiting Beliefs. This group is dangerous and uses cruel and unusual tactics to elude capture.

Arrest Report: At long last, Limiting Beliefs surrendered today. The standoff lasted for years but ended abruptly when its victims **woke up** and realized they were **being controlled** by the gang. It took some **counsel** and **encouragement** to bring them out, but they finally came out of hiding and were escorted to captivity.

3. Wanted: Procrastination

Considered dangerous to all who are trying to reach goals, this criminal causes extreme mental backups, delays, or the rescheduling of important events. Common MO includes the excessive use of these words and phrases: But, I Can't, I'll do it later, I have plenty of time, I thrive under pressure, I can reschedule, he or she will understand, I'll fake it until I make it, Stop nagging me, and I overslept. Procrastination has close ties to both Fear and Limiting Beliefs and is a habitual offender with a previous record a mile long.

Arrest Report: Procrastination was taking a nap in an abandoned building when officers apprehended it. The low energy thug actually asked if they could come back later for the arrest, but **precise action, time management skills, Completing Purpose**, and

quality decision-making pushed it to its jail cell where it could not harm anyone again.

4. Wanted: Overwhelm

Overwhelm is extremely cruel and kills its victims by burying or drowning them in a huge mass of dread and impending responsibility. This perpetrator attacks in waves with feelings of inferiority, stress, depression, anxiety, and even thoughts of suicide. This culprit is to be handled with caution and care. Its victims may be sensitive and erratic, and unwilling to walk away from their situations. Overwhelm has lots of friends around town. It is intimate with Procrastination, Fear, and Limiting Beliefs.

Arrest Report: Overwhelm was carefully apprehended today after the victim was made to **rest, reevaluate responsibility, Self-Soothe**, and **practice saying no**. It was a delicate operation that ended well.

5. Wanted: Lack of Confidence and Pride

True thieves, Lack of Confidence and Pride work as a team to steal momentum and leave their victims feeling helpless and as though they can't move forward without acquiring more knowledge, money, credibility, and things. Victims actually invite this criminal team in with thoughts of not being good enough and hiding their true selves. They hide deep within their victims, making capture tricky and time-consuming.

Arrest Report: The Lack of Confidence and Pride criminal team was brought down today after officers found them keeping a brilliant woman from being everything she could be. The woman had a series of puncture wounds to her self-confidence caused by the constant poking of the ruthless team. She was moved to a safe location where she received, **encouragement**, **praise**, **rewards for effort**, and **acceptance**.

I hope you enjoyed that at least as much as I did writing it . . .

CHAPTER TWELVE

A Little Passion
Goes A Long Way

"Passion is contagious, and when you have the courage to share your passion for life with those around you, it can inspire others to find the path to their dreams!

– MICHELE DEVILLE

Passion—A word with powerful energy and promise. It brings lovers together. It wins wars. It creates fine art and literature. It generates money, and it performs miracles. Those who embrace it have the potential to do all of the above and more. What are you constantly drawn to do that gives that blissful feeling of accomplishment and joy? Though your passions and your Purpose may not be a perfect match or the best of friends, it's likely they at least meet for coffee on occasion.

Keep in mind, though, there are passions that serve you and others well and those that don't. Just as the honorable, passionate woman brings beauty and love to the table, her counterpart, the selfish, greedy (equally passionate) gal can ruin lives faster than you can say desperate housewives. Is Your Passion Honorable and serving of others? In a perfect world, I could give you a perfect answer, but we all know that's not our present state as a species. So, instead, I will give you the best answer I know: It depends on what you believe is honorable. And, in that perfect world, we would all understand the legitimacy of honor. It is simple and really does fit in a nutshell: **Love**. If what you desire is driven by love, if it is knit from a yarn of joy, peace, and all things that serve, it's honorable.

Acting from a place of love and intuition honors not only you but all of mankind. Secondly, it makes room for you. That also means you won't fight tooth and nail to express or work within your passion. Furthermore, others notice you can't stop talking about it with a broad natural smile on your face. It expands your world and makes your heart beat faster.

A word of warning: Don't be surprised if, around the time you get this figured out, some challenging events unfold. It's like an initiation test that checks up on your intentions. *Do you really believe you can do this? Are you sure?* Not to worry, though, the initial trial period passes as soon as you push through it and make a commitment that nothing will hold you back from being who you are.

In a previous chapter we talked about manifesting your

desires. This wonderful process is the beginning of fulfilling your Dreams. Once you use it and realize you have power to change your life, infinite possibilities reveal themselves to you on a regular basis—one Dream at a time . . . or many. Suddenly, you say "yes" to your Dreams, instead of "no." You become the person you were meant to be simply by acting on the passions within your being. Purpose, passion, and Dreams amalgamate to create a solid platform for you.

I believe there is a distinct correlation between meeting your basic needs by honorable means and fulfilling Dreams and Purpose—just as for our friend, the butterfly. Her hunger and thirst drive her to the field of flowers where she fulfills a larger destiny. Our passion, Dreams, and need to be somebody in this world drive us to Purpose. Interesting, isn't it? See how it all makes perfect sense? How it flows with ease and continuity? Like a perfect cup of fresh brewed coffee. That's how it should be for each one of us. When it's not, a wire is disconnected somewhere. Something is out of place.

Com-passion Is Just as Important

"Some people think only intellect counts: knowing how to solve problems, knowing how to get by, knowing how to identify an advantage and seize it. But the functions of intellect are insufficient without courage, love, friendship, compassion and empathy."

I once heard true compassion defined as a person

doing something for another without being attached to the outcome of the situation. In other words, if you help someone, you don't do it because you believe it will create a certain result for that person or yourself. This really is a novel idea. Most people do things for others because they believe certain changes will occur—a perspective to which we've grown accustomed. Therefore, detaching ourselves from results is really difficult. For me, it is hard because I am results driven. That said, I still believe compassion is about connecting, not making something or someone change to fit our liking. Here's an example: I pray for my friend, and I do it because I want and expect her to get well. What happens if she doesn't get well? What if she dies instead? What then? True compassion is creating the atmosphere for what is best for the other person or situation to happen, not what we want or expect to transpire. Maybe she wanted to die . . . maybe it was her time to die. It's not up to us to decide the outcome for others. We don't have that sort of control. I realized that our own desires for a certain conclusion give unjust permission for us to judge where another person or situation is, that we have to somehow affect change on this person or unfair thing that's happening. Judgment attracts judgment . . . not something I want more of in my life.

Another example is easily seen in people asking for advice or critique on a creative project. Do we give our opinions because we want them to see things our way, or do we do it simply to give freely of ourselves as integral parts of the universe? We've become such a competitive society that I wonder if it isn't too late to change what's been programmed into us for too long now. We want what benefits us, even if it's not in a selfish way. It somehow benefits us if that woman we prayed for lives and is healed of her illness. It benefits us if that guy we gave advice to adheres to our creative thoughts and ideas. It makes us feel useful and proud. But, think about it for a moment: Are we compassionately understanding others and where they are when we project our opinions and needs into the situation?

Compassion is an emotion that is connected to pure human spirit and will. It's not something we should consider lightly or throw around with everything we do. Think of it as opportunity—one that shows unconditional love and desire to share our pure souls with others. No expectations. No gimmicks. No set results. Just a gift. It's like a bubble: We initiate it with action; it floats away with no real direction. It's free to go wherever it pleases, to pop or fly away into the heavens. No matter what it does, we find joy in creating it and watching it join this universe. Just think what we women could show the world with this kind of understanding of others and ourselves, if we could give of ourselves without expectations for the outcome concerning money, praise, recognition, success, friends, joy, satisfaction, gain, more referrals, followers, and clients.

Having a deep compassion for yourself and for others is also a prerequisite to forgiveness—an important topic we will discuss next. I completely believe that it is our agendas and need to be right that fuels our *flaming conflicts* with other people. Compassion leads to forgiveness, and forgiveness leads to freedom to fulfill Dreams.

CHAPTER THIRTEEN

Unforgiveness: A Major Roadblock

"Forgiveness is the fragrance that the violet sheds on the heel that has crushed it."

— MARK TWAIN

Allow me to be blunt (again): Unforgiveness is a MAJOR cause of dysfunction in our lives, one that steals Dreams. The sad thing is that most people don't realize they hold grudges, judge, and downright hate other people. These negative fixations could very well stem from events decades past. That's a lot of time to hold on to something that really only hurts you. We've all been hurt at some point, so let's get real here: YOU NEED TO HEAR THIS!

Think of unforgiveness as a nasty accident on the highway that blocks traffic in both directions. Yes, it's a HUGE mess! Nothing moves forward. Nothing goes through. Nothing passes the wreckage and emergency vehicles. You are upset, frustrated and have no idea when things will get back to normal. Your day is in shambles. What if that "mess" was in your way every single day of your life? Maybe it is and you don't know it. Well, I'm sending you an emergency vehicle to clear the road.

Clearing Past Offenses

Think about someone who has hurt you. Have you released him or her from the anger you feel? Have you released yourself from the pain? I know these questions may not make any sense to you, especially if you didn't realize you had a problem. Don't worry about understanding right now. Just know that allowing yourself to think about these offenses will help you let go of negative emotions that hold you back from being that beautiful butterfly that fulfills Purpose and gets everything she needs to survive.

The Forgiveness Payoff

Forgiving others is a conscious choice and action. It's not something that just happens because you're a nice or spiritual person. Whenever you have a choice, you must present intention or script your thoughts and actions before implementation. People do things, including forgiving others, because they get something out of it. This also means by not forgiving others you are likely getting—or think you're getting—something out of it, as well.

How does unforgiveness affect me? Good question. It really has everything to do with emotional patterns and a dialog that keeps looping in your head every time you encounter a certain situation. It could be your controlling mother or your untrustworthy partner who triggers an automatic response from you. The mechanisms that control your feelings and actions are programmed to allow maximum benefit to you in every situation. As I said in the previous paragraph, we do things and act certain ways because there is a Payoff for us. If you have residual wounds and issues from your past, you likely are reacting to current situations in a way that protects you from feeling an old pain. Are you following me? These patterns may divert you from your Dreams or stop them altogether.

Holding on to Past Hurts

Let's say your parents divorced when you were a child. A part of you blames them for destroying your family and the security that you felt. Suddenly, you are left with dark, unresolved feelings toward them. As a child, you don't know how to deal with these emotions. You simply want them to go away and for things to be what you consider normal. Well, they won't just magically go away until they are dealt with. Unfortunately, that doesn't usually happen until you reach a mature age, if even then. So here you are—an adult woman who has possibly been in many bad relationships and wonder why. In this case, your mother and father's or caretaker's example was the first of a love relationship. With that foundational coupling in disarray, you likely have problems relating in love relationships presently. The extent of your issues depends on how seriously you were hurt and how much of that pain has followed you into adulthood.

Do you see how unforgiveness hurts you? Let me add this disclaimer here:

Just because you forgive someone doesn't necessarily mean you will stop having negative thoughts and feelings. It certainly doesn't mean you will stop hurting completely.

You need to reread that statement until you get it. I don't want you to get tripped up on your own human nature. We are not perfect (in case you didn't notice). I have a laundry list of people I have forgiven, but I still deal with negative thoughts and regrets when I least expect. Just make sure disturbing thoughts don't outweigh the pleasant ones. If they do, you have to wonder if you really did forgive. Also, there are other more in-depth models to work through to release trapped emotions and pain. I use techniques like The Emotion Code, Reiki, and Intuitive Readings all the time with clients, family, and myself to assist in shedding emotional baggage.

Speak It Out

The unfortunate example of a broken home is just one of many I could detail, but I think you get the point. Whatever your personal event is, revisiting it may make you feel emotional, like crying or throwing something. This is the time to let it out (safely and healthfully, please! Don't take it out on Grandmother's fine china). Speak out or journal what you want to say to that person even if they aren't really in front of you. If you are ready, verbally say the words, "I forgive you_____for_____." Fill in the blanks with a name and the details of the event. Ask God or your Devine Source to help you forgive the people who have hurt you. You need to release the pain and allow yourself to start fresh no matter what the circumstances are or who the person is. You deserve the chance to be the best you. Not to mention, you will infuse positive energy into your life, your Dreams, and the relationships you have now.

Forgive Yourself

Forgiving *yourself* for non-serving past acts is another monumental task because we can be so hard on ourselves. We may allow self-loathing to continue due to a belief that it somehow motivates us to be a better person, that it gives us some kind of edge. In reality, it's doing the opposite. Letting go of personal mistakes clears the path to reaching and fulfilling Dreams and Purpose. And, remember, this works both ways. Just as you've been hurt, you've hurt others. Recall times when you were the one not serving humanity well. If you're ready, and if it's possible, go to those people and ask them to forgive you. Rid yourself of this burden. Promote yourself to the life you want.

This subject is so serious you might consider seeking help if you're not making progress. I am always available to answer specific questions about forgiveness, so please don't hesitate to connect with me via the contact information at the end of this book. Don't underestimate the power of this exercise. This step is HUGE! Take your time, as this incredible part of your Journey is worth more than you know. I'll be honest with you, it could take days, weeks, and even months to see the benefits from your efforts. Don't get discouraged, though. You're on the right track. When you accomplish it, you will know it. Choose forgiveness as a Journey lifestyle. You will naturally be a more fulfilled woman with dynamic relationships.

CHAPTER FOURTEEN

Here Comes the Judge

"The only justice is to follow the sincere intuition of the soul, angry or gentle. Anger is just, and pity is just, but judgment is never just."
– D.H. LAWRENCE

I focused on forgiveness in the previous chapter. Now, I would like to expand on the somewhat parallel issue of judging others—similar to unforgiveness in that the consequences can manifest as a life roadblock. Judging others is devastating to our emotional and even physical well-being. Whenever we point a finger at or criticize someone, we damage a part of ourselves, considering the energetic connection. The process of sowing and reaping or Karma is unmistakably alive and well on planet earth. It doesn't matter what you call it, the fact is it's a spiritual law that doesn't stop working just because you don't want to acknowledge or believe it.

The Experience of Judgment

Here's an example: If you nonchalantly judge another for being overweight or unsightly in appearance, chances are you or someone you love will be judged for the very same things. I know it sounds odd and almost unbelievable, but it's real. I've tested this philosophy on my own life, and I've clearly see the ripple effect. Every problem or conflict I deal with today has a link to something or someone I judged in the past. Because this pattern starts at a young age, finding yourself out of control by the time you reach your adulthood is likely. I know I did. Checking yourself daily is the only way to make sure your personal gavel doesn't fall on innocent victims. Judgment is another ten car pile-up on the freeway—one you don't want to be detained by, or worse. And, yes, your Dreams may be in the custody of one such disaster.

Another Visit to the Past

Think about the major issues of your life. What would you like to change for the better? Pull out your Life Area list from earlier. These categories are all important aspects of your life and ones that can cause stress and concern when things aren't going well. I'm not saying that 100% of your problems are from judging others . . . just consider the concept. First, revisit how you saw your parents, grandparents or caretakers. How did they raise you? Were they kind and fair or were they cold and distant? More than likely, they were somewhere in the middle. No matter what your special case is, you have—whether you like it or not—developed some sort of judgment based on your experiences and emotions.

It could be your parents were horrible at handling money and, likely, you paid some of the bill for their issues—disappointed by lack and being told "no" too often, feeling neglected. These continual feelings developed into judgments and followed you right into your adulthood. If this is the case, you may now have some financial difficulties for which your own children or others may be judging you. It's a nasty cycle that someone has to break. That person is you!

True Confessions

This situation requires quite a bit of cleanup of past attitudes and judgments but also strict attention to the present. You release judgments much like you forgive. A verbal confession like "I have judged _____ for _____ and release him or her (and myself) from this judgment and its consequences" sends the message to the universe that you are serious and ready to make changes. This is the time to turn to your spiritual strength to help you break this cycle of negative power over your life. In addition to your private, verbal confession, go to your loved ones and tell them of the judgments you have carried. Ask them to forgive you. I think you'll be delighted by the positive outcome from this experience. Don't be surprised if long overdue apologies and reconciliation occurs. Additionally, you will see some breakthrough in that particular area of your life that may hold the key to a long-awaited Dream.

Lifestyle of Kindness

Turning to the present, be aware of your thoughts and reaction to others around you. Passing quick judgments on our fellow humans is harsh and unwarranted. Truly, we have no right to judge anything about another person. Yes, appearance, social and financial status, education, and employment are out there and may seem to ask for approval or disapproval, but it doesn't mean we should be critics. Unfortunately, our culture is flawed in its need to judge, categorize, and provoke competition. If you point the finger, remember, it's pointing right back at you only more harshly.

Analyze your feelings if you notice a continual pattern of negative thoughts for a particular person or group of people. It could be a root of bitterness that runs deep in your soul. This might be the time to seek professional help for your continued Journey. Sometimes the human mind hides extremely painful events to protect us from further turmoil. It's an instinct to keep us functioning. Remembering too much might disturb that balance. You could feel some emotional strain from this exercise, as it will bring up some old garbage. Journaling is crucial as you work through this stage of progress.

People generally do the best they can at living, according to their knowledge level and situation. If only our unkind thoughts and judgments really did make people change, or better yet, make us better. If only we could just will that street person to a bath and a job with our rolling eyes and disgusted heart and, in return, we would get a promotion and a nice spa treatment. I know this sounds silly but think about it in simple terms: What is really accomplished by judging others? Remember, a "reaction" happens from every "action" whether we like it or not. We have to change if we want the world to change. Stop the tragic ridicule! Spread some kindness and love for a week and see how fast your Dreams unfold and the Payoff comes.

CHAPTER FIFTEEN

Choose Happiness-Choose Love

"Many persons have a wrong idea of what constitutes true happiness. It is not attained through self-gratification but through fidelity to a worthy purpose."

– HELEN KELLER

I've often wondered why some women are just naturally happy and others are chronically distraught or depressed. Is there really that much difference between the circumstances of each to cause such dramatic opposition? I mean, really, don't we all have good days, bad days, bills, kids that hit home runs, health issues, triumphs and tragedies? So, if we are all more alike than we think, why the attitude difference?

I'd like to point out four keys that I've discovered. I use these to remind myself and my clients that true happiness is a choice—an active one. But before starting, rate your general happy-level on a scale from 1 to 10. Write it in your journal so you can track your progress.

Now while reading this chapter, ask yourself these questions :

If I incorporate these simple actions into my life, how will my state of mind be affected?

Will I be happier?

Is there a reason being happy is so difficult?

Am I unhappy because I haven't seen my Dreams come true, or have my Dreams not come true because I'm always unhappy?

Happiness, joy, bliss, peace, and love are all emotions that fuel Dream and life fulfillment. I believe that they may even be the closest connection we can ever have with God or any spiritual source. But what happens when none of these show up regularly? Well, the opposite: sadness, anger, anxiety, hate, dis-satisfaction— a life that lacks substance and conscious Purpose. While you can do many things to add a little joy to your day, there are three things in particular that are more than quick pick-me-ups. They are lifestyle adjustments that move you (and the universe) to actively change your life.

Thing #1: Regular Exercise and Stretching

I know it's been said, and said, and said some more, but did you pay attention? Did I pay attention? Maybe. Maybe not. Two points with this: First, regular exercise (3 + times per week) produces endorphins (feel-good hormones) that actually combat depression and melancholy. And secondly, it keeps your body in great shape! In other words, if you know you look and feel good, your attitude is *WAY* more likely to be positive.

Actively pursuing fitness puts your mind, body, and spirit in a ready position to receive and process whatever comes into your life.

More specifically, some forms of exercise, like Kundalini Yoga and Tai Chi will produce significant change in your emotional and physical state by disciplining you to slow down and enjoy each moment. These techniques may not be for you, but you will never know until you try them. Ultimately, the important thing is that you find a fitness routine you enjoy and works for your life.

Thing #2: Introspection and Retrospection

Taking the time to reflect on your day before you go to bed is one way to combat confusion, anxiety, and ill-feelings about another person or situation. I find the best way to begin introspection is to ask myself a question that is not easily answered by "yes" or "no." Write it down in a journal, and start spilling your guts. Don't forget to recognize disturbing emotions and even choices that may have hurt others. Admitting fault and taking responsibility for your actions, relationships, and words brings positive life change. Blaming others always ends up biting you in the ass one way or another. After all, only you can truly change you and your life for the better. Only you can make your Dreams come to pass.

Thing #3: Creativity

Whether you think so or not, we are all creative beings. We are wired to see, develop, and master creative abilities within ourselves. This doesn't mean you have to take up oil painting or sculpturing. Creativity is expressed in endless forms and mediums. With infinite possibilities available, don't struggle with trends or what you think others would like. Be yourself . . . always. If you have trouble getting started, think about what you loved to do as a child. What made you the happiest? What types of things did you make and think about frequently? Sometimes just being with children, I mean really *BE-ING* with them, gives a dose of spontaneity and candor—just the ingredients you need to create freely and without self-consciousness.

Thing #4: Live In the Moment

The past is behind you, the future is unknown. There is no time like the present to be you. When you spend too much time comparing the *now* to days gone by, you'll wake up one day and find that years have passed while you were busy trying to make your life live up to a long-ago happy place that should have been left right where it belongs . . . in the past. Frankly, I call this tragedy a "pain in the neck" because you can't stop turning around to look at a time that will never be again. Hello, neck strain. Hello, life strain. Oddly enough, it's equally damaging to always look too far into the future. I believe in setting goals and being mindful of the future, but excessive waiting for your proverbial ship to come in order to be happy is no way to live. There will always be a bigger and better "ship" out there. You might as well decide to be happy now, in the present, no matter what the circumstances.

The Butterfly Payoff

The Message of Love

Many spiritual leaders and masters, including Jesus, Buddha, and the present Dalai Lama proclaim the message of love and peace . . . period. No ands. No ifs. No buts. Love serves and presents all its wonder on a proverbial silver platter. Meaning, if we give our best love, the universe will give us its. Even if you don't agree with the religious doctrine the followers of these iconic leaders teach and live by, the spiritual law still applies. Application of love and peace is the key to understanding and experiencing their benefits.

Most people have a cell phone or at least a computer. So, I expect you've downloaded a few useful apps. Well, those apps are on your mobile device or computer until you remove them. And they run in the background whether you choose to open them or not. Love is like that. It's a choice. You either open and use it or leave it alone to run uselessly in the background, in the dormant part of your life.

Every person on this planet has the potential to love and be loved. We are a love-***able*** species. It's in our DNA, our innate instinct. It's when we choose to ignore this miraculous gift, we go against the very fiber of our beings, of creation. Failure to choose love always results in a disruption of life itself. Have you ever wondered why crime, sickness, poverty, and disasters corrupt our world? I believe these are the result of millions of people rejecting the spiritual law of love.

I once met a man named Ed. Now, Ed wasn't extraordinarily handsome by the world's standard, didn't wear fine clothing and had no magical way of speaking. But when he spoke, Ed forever changed my life.

"*I love everyone I've met in my life as much as I ever did,*" he matter-of-factly uttered over a beer. Ed went on to say his claim included two ex-wives. He didn't mean he was still pining, but that he had a general, everlasting love for them. Ed made this choice to not hate, belittle, or feel anger toward his ex-wives or any other human being who had crossed his Journey path. I literally sat dumbfounded, waiting for him to explain how he could possibly do such a supernatural thing. Ed understands the message of love. And, in doing so, he lives a peaceful life free from stress and even disease.

Focus on Your Relationships, Not Being Right

Humans get into fights. They disagree. They ponder for days, even weeks, to prepare confrontational addresses for those they love. Do we really only hurt the ones we love? That kind of conflict is deadly to happiness and the fulfillment of Dreams. It's not that you should never enter into a debate or disagreement that, of course, is a human right. However, what if there was a secret way to live your life with joy, love, and peace that allowed you and others to be themselves without conflict? There is. It's called indifference (another nugget Ed offered me). We see pain and hardships all around us. We all experience both at times. Being indifferent allows you to live through these times without the stress and strain so often at the forefront of conflict. In other words, if you can't change it, leave it alone. Find a neutral emotion. It's okay to let some things go, to walk away with your head held high, knowing that you didn't allow the situation to affect you in a non-serving way.

- **Be aware of your thoughts.** Don't allow yourself to get caught up in your own drama. We can create a world with our minds. What kind are you working on?

- **Do everything out of love.** Giving above and beyond to help others and by serving them is a sure way to bring joy into your life. Do also remember to love and care for yourself first.

- **Be grateful.** Each day write or speak out what you are thankful for in your life. Tell those whom you love they are important. The rewards are endless.

What Problems Are You Here To Solve?

I ask this question not to get you focused on the world's problems but the opposite: the solutions. You have answers to specific issues all around you whether you choose to acknowledge them or not. And, these answers are rooted at the core of your Purpose and your Dreams. Your reveries aren't supposed to just wallow in your mind or on a "to do" list. They are meant to be fulfilled by universal design. The deeper you go into your Dreams, the more fulfilling they become to you and the world. If you think about starving children all the time and even get choked up when those heart-wrenching commercials come on, you may be getting clues to do something to remedy the problem. It may be as simple as giving a small amount of money to the cause, or as complicated as setting up an entire foundation to support a community. No matter what your part is, you owe it to yourself and others to follow through with your vision of change.

I've never known a woman who didn't have an idea to change something. We are built to bring love, peace, and joy to our families and society in general. How we do this is as unique as we are. Now, can you understand how important my question is? If you truly answer it with love and integrity, you will take your first step to fulfilling your own Dreams. **What problems are you here to solve?**

CHAPTER SIXTEEN

Validation

"You are not validated by what you do but by who you are."

Think about the butterfly again for a moment. She is a magical creature that even without any specific action is desired and respected by the world. Even if she just sits on a branch with no intention of wandering into the meadow and accidentally pollenating the flowers, she is validated by simply being her beautiful self. Fortunately, all living species *DO* have Purpose and the innate drive to fulfill it. Humans are no exception. We are quite able to accomplish many things, but that's not what validates us in the Universe. We are also magical, divine creatures who *ARE*, and that is enough. So, I guess what we *do* is the painting or decoration—not necessary, but it makes life much more interesting, more colorful. The reason for this chapter is not to tell you Dreams and actions don't matter. I just want you to first acknowledge the value of *YOU* as you are right now without a list of accomplishments to set you apart.

If you don't realize the value in yourself now, you run the risk of never seeing it, even after achieving some or all of your Dreams. You are valid no matter what you do or don't get done today, tomorrow, or have done in the past. After all, you may be fulfilling your Dream or that of someone else by just being alive.

Years ago, I went to a vocal coach for training and feedback. I remember telling her how I wanted to sing, the style and genre in which I wanted to master. She told me that was great and all but that I had to strip down what style I already had and solidify the basics of my vocal instrument. I had to build on a firm foundation. Though I wanted to do all the fancy riffs and vocal gymnastics, I couldn't do them without being sound where I was. I had to validate myself as an instrument before I made fancy music. Just as we have to validate ourselves as women before we change the world or fulfill a Dream.

Dangerous Motivation

There is a danger in only seeking Dreams to impress others or to somehow gain notoriety, credibility and identity. I know most of you aren't doing this consciously. However, it could be a deep set need for praise or recognition that drives you subconsciously. It's dangerous because, if gone unchecked, it will destroy your ability to recognize your authentic self and her serving intentions. Not to mention, it will run you into the ground with stress and discontentment. The fact that you have your smile, your laugh, your special way of comforting others is what makes you, *YOU*. These and the many other facets of your being are components of a living soul—one that cannot be replaced or duplicated. Validation.

Credibility/Notoriety

I've seen many women struggle with self-acceptance and Dream-fulfillment because they didn't believe they had enough credibility in the world's eyes. Understand that this world is a conglomerate of money, resources, and people who are all trying to survive and make their mark on the world. Getting noticed in that gigantic pool is not easy, unless you do a cannonball and splash everyone in the vicinity. Not a bad idea but most don't have the desire or guts to go through with such an act of complete disruption or the resources to handle the ripple effect. But, hey, if you do . . . go for it! First, you have to ask yourself what it is your trying to accomplish and why. Remember, I said that your Dream will make room for you? Well, I'm not sure if that applies to forceful actions of body wielding into water! Maybe you should stick to a more subtle approach at first.

Once you get solid about who you are as a woman, you begin to see just how you fit into the world and what contributions are your thing. And, the universe moves mountains to make those things happen. Why? Because it's a system, a design, a collective effort. Credibility comes from natural acceptance of who we are—a confidence that we matter in the big scheme of things, no matter where we come from or how small we feel. Do you know the world could not function without the existence of billions of microscopic species? It's simply their drive to survive that, in turn, makes room for another to do the same. This system is in place at all levels of life.

One morning, I was sitting out on my patio meditating, when I felt this overwhelming sting on my forearm. I struggled to keep my focus and regain the peace I had obtained. My curiosity and the fact that it really hurt got the better of me. I looked at my arm and was shocked to find an insect so small that I could hardly see it. That little bug not only caused physical harm to me but made me change my course. It affected something much larger than itself. Aren't nature's lessons awesome! So, don't get all depressed because you think you don't matter and you're too small to make a difference. Nonsense! Credibility comes when you are yourself! As far as being known and admired, that's another level on the food chain—one that comes after inserting yourself into life (the pool) repeatedly . . . cannonball or not.

People, especially women, are natural news spreaders. We tend to tell everyone about what and who makes us feel good (or bad). The good news is that anyone trying to accomplish something of value can utilize this natural process. When you make people feel good about themselves, they give you the recognition you deserve. And if this notoriety is a part of your Dream, it will happen if you take the necessary steps to get there. Before anything happens, you have to get yourself out there to be noticed. If that means finally getting on a social network or joining a women's book club, then get busy! You won't make those ripples hiding in your sunroom or office. That said, I have a perfect story about this very topic. My dear colleague and friend, Sharon Nicholas, experienced a remarkable change in the fulfillment of her Dreams after overcoming her self-doubt and fears concerning her ability to present her gifts to the world. She had quite an enlightening experience when unexpected attention came from all over when she opened up and shared her Dream with other women. Allow Sharon's story to encourage you as you walk on your own Journey to Purpose.

Sharon Nicholas' Story

For as many years as I can remember, I've had big dreams. Allowing myself to dream big takes continual letting go, releasing fears, embracing possibilities and opening myself up to the "what ifs" in life. I give myself permission to envision my dream life, to dream bigger and think outside the box. We all deserve to live out our passions! We all dream, but not every woman chooses to fight for and live out her dreams.

I've had passing thoughts of projects I'd love to launch. I've also made choices to either move forward and pursue these dreams or to let my own self-doubt and insecurities take over. I'm no stranger to letting go of dreams and ideas and watching them frequently get replaced by the reasons why I can't realize them.

For many years, I wanted to build a magazine. My inspiration: Helen Gurley Brown, the editor-in-chief of Cosmopolitan, who is actually my cousin's cousin. Having a full blown magazine was not a small dream. The notion decorated my mind as a teen, but I often let myself waffle back and forth on the idea. I knew when this desire wouldn't leave me alone that it might be my ultimate vocation. Realizing that it wasn't going away, I often thought it might be time to take action and make it happen.

The aspect of contemplating facts overwhelmed me. The dream and building it took over my thought process. My thoughts were a soup mixed with excitement and the reality of my fears. The cost, time and developing the knowledge level to accomplish my dream were all valid concerns and frequently held me back from taking action steps. I let self-doubt take over most of my life; however, with time comes wisdom, as they say. Focusing on the statistics of women in the writing industry also made me feel better. I discovered that confidence as a woman writer blossoms later in life. We frequently start writing much later than our male counterparts.

The self-development steps to change my thinking happened over time. Taking the time to have heart-to-heart discussions about my idea with other women was one of the best things I have ever done. Women entrepreneurs, authors, writers, journalists and personal friends all supported me tremendously. Thoughts of launching my project changed while speaking with others. They truly helped me overcome my fears and encouraged me to follow my passions, to live my dreams.

Studying other women and their careers also opened my eyes. How they managed to embrace their passions and turn them into successful careers became an important key for me. I was fascinated by their career stories that detailed where they started and how far they had come. I realized that it was a process to build their careers in layers over many years. Seeing how others took their past skills to new levels and, at the same time, expand on their natural talents inspired me.

Upon deep self-examination of my own insecurities and some self-talk, my fears, self-doubts and worries eased in time. Reflecting on how to overcome each one and pushing myself out there to start a project was a challenge, though. In fact, at times it became an in-surmountable challenge to me as a shy person. Once my focus moved away from the "can't" mentality and focused on "how to" thoughts, things began to change and unfold before my eyes! Time researching and building replaced time spent dwelling on the reasons I could not do it. Once the dream of the magazine started to become a reality, the time spent was a labor of love. Amazingly, people stepped up to help which was affirming in itself. It became a bigger project than I first imaged, though. The beginning was incredible! I realized my true path while others saw my passion clearly and volunteered their time to help me. I learned by reaching out to others that my passion for writing was my true vocation.

Once the magazine was underway, I felt I had overcome both lifelong challenges of mental clarity and physical execution. To fulfill a lifelong passion is something every woman should do at least once in her life. When I found my true path, others followed. People learned of my project . . . more people than I'd ever imagined. It was astonishing to look at my dream unfolding. In some ways, though, I wasn't surprised on a deeper level. I spent my days dreaming of it for many years. Another aspect of living my dream was that other dimensions unfolded. My dream project spurred sister projects, and the project itself opened doors I couldn't envision at first.

Thinking back now, I realize the acceptance of my fears was an important part of the process. Time spent reflecting on my goals and allowing myself to get excited about my future scared me, but it was a process of growth and development I had to experience. Once I started living more for the future, the doors of possibility opened. I gave permission for everything to unfold.

It takes many steps to build our greatest visions: thought, planning, execution, and the launch of our project. All these steps can seem overwhelming and tedious while you're working on them. But with faith, commitment and belief in ourselves we can accomplish any goal. We all are designed to become our greatest selves because we are all capable of accomplishing something special in our lives. Don't doubt this. We all have unique gifts and talents. Our job is to embrace them and convey them to the world. Strangely, some women frequently avoid doing just that.

Out of fear, we often avoid fostering and flourishing these talents. Our natural abilities sometimes seem too easy to execute. These natural talents may not feel like a real career so we fail to pursue them. It's a "someday" way of thinking that keeps our dreams and projects out into the future. We self-talk ourselves out of doing what we should really be doing with our lives.

I had to change myself to get where I am today. I faced my need to learn and develop myself head on. Creating your greatest life is not for the weak of heart, it's for those who are up for the challenge and don't mind being in an unknown space. My end result has been extremely gratifying and confirmed that my dream could become a reality. Believe you can do it, and you will!

As Walt Disney said, *"All our dreams can come true, if we have the courage to pursue them."* He practiced what he preached, as he pursued his dream: Co-founding Walt Disney Productions. We can all do the same, if we have the conviction that the pursuit of our dreams is as mandatory as breathing.

Like everyone who wants to build community and a support network, Sharon created and built relationships with people who eventually helped her launch her Dream. It was a process that required time and energy. Sharon went through these important stages before the floodgates opened up!

The first step to creating a following or public credibility is to give more than you take. When we share value with others we are actually giving little parts of ourselves to the world. These parts are the micro-organisms that may stay under the radar but have a huge impact on how things survive and thrive. I am a woman who believes that even the most insignificant acts of kindness and mere words can and will change the world as a whole. That's why I always encourage women to speak out and share their stories with at least one person. If you do this often enough it will build a foundation of character that people notice and share. This is especially helpful for women who aspire to be messengers, coaches, authors, public speakers, and teachers on a broad scale.

The second thing that gets you on the map of public recognition is building relationships. This is a task that takes time and sincerity. You can't just barge into someone's life or social media page and demand attention or a thumbs up. It's a long road of perseverance that you have to be willing to travel. Again, it's back to how you make people feel that stirs them enough to evoke a reaction. Do yourself and your Dreams a favor: be kind, gentle, and honest. What if I'm shy, you ask? Well, you do what you can.

The Butterfly Payoff

Sharon did. Take baby steps if you have to. Meet new people in the company of those you know. Ask your best friends to introduce you to their groups. Just one new person in your life could be the one who helps you get your Dream moving in the right direction. Open your mouth and stop making excuses for yourself. You will find people to help you build your Dream if you don't give up.

One last tip for catching the world's eye: **do often that which you seldom do now.** This will literally change your life in all areas if you apply it. Think about how much better you could make your life if you frequently repeated serving acts like, encouraging a friend, exercising, giving, saving, eating good foods, saying no, saying yes, or just giving yourself a break. Now apply this to the fulfillment of your Dream. See what I mean? You can't go wrong. It works every time! Kind of one of those wash-rinse-repeat things.

Though your Dreams may not involve crowds (or even five people for that matter) you still need to know how to network and ask for help when you need it. I am a part of a group on a popular social network that offers a place for members to share their Dreams and ask for help with them. Total strangers chime in about your Dream and actually make suggestions or offer assistance in making it come true. I share a common goal with the founder of this group: we both want to help others fulfill their Dreams. Maybe you do too. Just remember to get out there into the world— the world where you and your Dream fit perfectly. This is the place where you receive your Payoff.

PART III

THE LIVING PAYOFF

CHAPTER SEVENTEEN

Seeing (Creating) It Through

"To everything there is a season, and a time to every purpose under the heaven; a time to be born, and a time to die; a time to plant, and a time to pluck up that which is planted; a time to weep, and a time to laugh; a time to mourn, and a time to dance."

– THE BIBLE, ECCLESIASTES 3:1, 2, 4(KJV)

You may be thinking about all of the steps it takes to actually get to the point where you experience some sort of Payoff in your life, and that is certainly okay. Though, I guess one extremely important point that would serve you here is this: You are already seeing, experiencing, hearing, loving or hating, ignoring, and altogether living your Payoff. I know you didn't expect me to say that. Well . . . I honestly didn't either. It's just that I've realized over the course of writing this book that there is no better experience than the one I'm having right this very minute. Each moment has a Payoff. Each thing has a season, a time, a Purpose, just like our beloved butterfly. That said, I will, however, share some deeper and more specific experiences you can expect from journeying to and through Purpose and Payoff.

The Flowers and Fruit Are Already There

You've spent your life collecting moments or, more accurately, living (or ignoring) them. Each one is a seed—an opportunity to create. I have spent much time in this book talking about how our actions produce reactions and how our thoughts and attitudes affect everything about our lives. It is my deepest desire that you understand how much potential you have to manifest everything you've ever imagined . . . just like a seed, it's inside of you. Within any seed is an orchard, a forest, a crop, and the same infinite potential resides inside you and me. We possess life beyond what we can see with our naked eye or comprehend in our minds—an amazing reality that has astounded philosophers, spiritual teachers, scientists, and all of humanity for as long as we've recorded history.

In order for you to grasp exactly what your personal Payoff is now and will become, you must open your mind and heart to the idea that you *do* create your life and the circumstances represented within it. It is being present in the flow of one moment to the next that builds the perfect bridge to your wildest Dreams and fulfillment of *YOU*. I didn't say "fulfillment of Purpose" there because it is now time for you to see that your Purpose as nothing more and nothing less than who you already are. (Sorry, I didn't want to tell you that in the beginning and spoil all the fun.) And your *Payoff* is always present within that understanding.

The Butterfly Payoff

Creating Your World
Is Living Your Purpose

It is easy to see why many people go searching for Purpose and glorious Payoffs outside of themselves. They look at others and compare their experience with what they see others achieving. A fantastical game begins—one that throws them into a circus of trying to be better, richer, faster, more popular, smarter, and powerful. You DO *NOT* want a ticket to this show! This is a masculine performance of pride, greed, and power. And, yes, we live in this male dominated world, but it's time for a new show . . . a new game. And we are the stars! We are the divine feminine creators of life and harmony on so many levels. Why should it be any different for this personal development thing? It's not!

Think about how you become a mother. A seed is planted. She grows. She is nurtured. She expands some more until she finally outgrows her space, so she journeys. You labor. She emerges (though this process of birth differs for all, it generally produces the same results). You both have experienced not only Purpose but a distinct Payoff. Every bit of this happens by creative design. There is no comparing in this process, no prideful greed, no needless toil to make it something it's not. NO, it just is what it is. YOU and everything you create just are. Your world happens by imaginative design.

Are You Dreaming Big Enough?

One thing we can likely all relate to is that our beliefs about what is possible (our Dreams) get stuck sometimes. What do they get stuck in or on? Well, my beliefs about myself and my potential have been, at times, stuck in the worst quicksand-ish, mucky mud, stench-filled mind traps you could ever imagine. These prison-like places have kept me from Dreaming big at times. How about you? This place I've described, though only a fictional scene to paint a picture, can be just as dangerous to your future as if you were actually neck deep in a bog. Our minds have the capacity to make things real . . . all things, serving and non-serving. Don't you think if you expanded your mind a little where your Dreams are concerned, you just might see some amazing things happen for real? I challenge you.

The fact is, we tend to focus our lives on what we know, what we've experienced and use these templates as an outline for future endeavors. Don't we? Why? Because it's safe. We've been there before. But, guess what? It's a slimy, wasteland bog, devouring our Purpose and potential. Truthfully, we are all much stronger, smarter, wiser, and capable than we give ourselves credit for. Our Dreams are proof that we are here for a reason, that we do have the ability to make them come to pass. We wouldn't even come up with the ideas in the first place if that were not so. Can you believe that?

Clean Up the Bog

Yes, it can be done. Focus. Action. Time. Clarify. Acceptance. Treat. I just noticed the acronym spells FAT CAT . . . yes, I'm laughing at myself. It does sort of go with what I'm saying, though. Fat cats are usually happy, well fed, have leisure time to spend napping and playing. They get lots of attention. They enjoy life more than most. Sign me up! So, let's go through each of these <u>FAT CAT</u> steps and get our minds out of the stink zone, shall we?

- **Focus -** Sometimes things aren't always what they seem to be. Often we have to focus a little harder to see details in order to gain understanding. This is the beginning of the Journey to anywhere new. Focusing on the present environment and knowing where you are is the only way to get where you want to be. Look and see what surrounds you (people, skills, resources, tools, weapons, talents, etc.) and then assign them a Purpose or simply throw them out. **And, don't forget to write this all down in your journal.**

- **Action -** The realization of all that you have and all whom you presently are is the first step to cleaning things up. The second is putting those ideas into action. Yes, it's the work part. Remember up in the previous section where I said to "throw them out?" Digging crap up and heaving it out of your life will take some emotional and physical energy and consistency.

Obviously, getting rid of the old is necessary before anything new can enter into the picture. Not doing this first is one of the reasons women fail at implementing change and Dream plans. Once you get this icky part complete, you can then assign your assets to innovative projects and plans.

- **Time** - Give yourself time to make changes. And, give yourself time to rest. There is no rush to making your Dreams come true. It is a Journey, remember? Enjoy the time you have on the Journey and in every situation you find yourself. It's your life. Your Dream. Don't let anyone tell you that you've missed the boat or failed in some in-retractable way. It's never too late to Dream bigger and live those Dreams.

- **Clarify** - This is the time to make sure you haven't wandered off course and that what you've set out to do is what you *really . . . no, I mean REALLY* want. Course corrections will be much easier at this early stage than they would be later in the process. Habits are harder to break when they've been entertained for long periods of time. That's really how we get stuck in the BOG in the first place.

- **Acceptance** - Respect yourself for who and where you are. Accept that obstacles will present themselves, that things go awry but also accept that there is always a way to overcome them. Accept that these speed bumps could be a clue you need others in your life to help. Ask for help when you need it!

- **Treat -** For the love of God, give yourself a pat on the back (or a big chocolate bar) when you reach a goal or milestone. Most people love rewards for a job well done. Giving yourself a treat for accomplishing a goal causes a memory recall type of process in your brain. It remembers how pleasant doing well is and wants to feel that bliss again . . . and again.

Use this simple outline for digging out of the mind bog and Dreaming a little bigger as frequently as you need to, so your Payoff comes faster and looks like what you envisioned. You can be the FAT CAT woman you're meant to be in every area of your life with a little work and patience.

Acceptance of What Is (Indifference)

It's effortless to accept a coveted promotion, an award, an offer of support from a trusted friend, or an altogether perfect day. But when things don't go as you think they should, acceptance hides behind your mind's incessant need to make things better or perfect. Don't beat yourself up over this, as you've likely been practicing it your entire life without any challenge. Yeah, me too. It takes conscious effort to change old habits, and this one is a tough one.

Do you remember in a previous chapter when I spoke of indifference? It's a close cousin to acceptance.

Accepting all things as they are is really nothing more than deciding that they are neither good nor bad where your life is concerned. If you really think about it, how can we really classify a thing to be either when we can't see the whole picture of our lives? What seems bad one day may produce your greatest joy the next.

When the law of cause and effect are at play, things organically happen. Human beings are the only species on the planet that put labels of judgment on the events of their lives. I believe a more serving way to look at life is to consider each moment an opportunity to remember who you are. And in doing so, you will need to discover who you are not through your experiences. In other words, if you get a new job and you absolutely hate it, don't consider it a bad thing but an opportunity to understand yourself in a deeper way. If you can adopt this way of life, you will recognize the Payoffs more quickly and appreciate them when they do manifest.

The Journey Continues

On this magical Journey to Purpose and Payoff, you will experience every scope of emotion. At least I hope you do. It's necessary for us to travel through our lives, understanding that it is diverse and speckled with situations that challenge our plans, to say the least. This is the time to commit yourself to your life once and for all. Your mind will want to change a million times because it doesn't like to be outside of its comfort zone. It likes to do and think exactly what it has in the past. However, in order for you to continue your Journey with commitment, you will need to adjust your beliefs and old habits.

We've talked about this topic some in previous chapters, but I want to pull it all together here by saying this: It's okay to not be okay. Allow yourself the freedom to make choices even if they don't seem logical, perfect, or within your personal comfort zone. After all, you are drawn to that choice for some reason. Your Journey unfolds as you move . . . remember that.

Lisa Marie Rosati says, *"Imperfect action trumps in-action every time!"* Payoffs are everywhere, around every corner, behind every door. It's up to you to reveal what you've ultimately created.

CHAPTER EIGHTEEN

It's ALL About YOU!

"Your time is limited, don't waste it living someone else's life. Don't be trapped by dogma, which is living the result of other people's thinking. Don't let the noise of other's opinion drown your own inner voice. And most importantly, have the courage to follow your heart and intuition, they somehow already know what you truly want to become. Everything else is secondary."

– STEVE JOBS

We've all heard people ripping on others who seem to do only that which benefits themselves, right? And, at the time, you may have even agreed with the colorful names they called these people: selfish, manipulating, careless, narcissistic, lonely, bitch, bastard, and plenty of others I won't mention. Well, here's the thing: those individuals may not have connected to the greater good of mankind yet or even what it means to help out their neighbor, but they have connected to themselves.

147

Though I'm not condoning only doing that which serves you and you alone, I am suggesting that there is something these people can teach us about self-awareness.

These "selfish" ones are merely conducting life through the model they've set up in their lives. It's not wrong, it is just their awareness. One thing is for sure, they have the taking care of themselves thing down . . . something many of us do not. If we don't care for ourselves, then who will? And, if we don't meet our needs, how will we effectively meet the needs of others? We truly deny the world something every time we deny ourselves our deepest desires and Purpose. To me, that seems selfish.

Playing All Your Cards

In many card games, you play your best cards in hopes of winning the game (like the three of a kind with an ace kicker). If you play lower value cards, you could lose by the lack of even one single card. What if we are doing the same thing with our life hand by only playing our best and hiding our self-proclaimed low qualities? Not sure about you, but I've hidden some of my truth in hopes that people would accept me. This act makes life more about others than yourself by caring too much about what they think of YOU. Do you think this serves anyone in the long run?

Bringing our dim weaknesses to the light is one way to help them grow into strengths. In the case of gathering your Payoffs, it is vital. Any darkness among our thoughts and feelings toward ourselves—though it has

Purpose—if left for a long period of time can hinder your inner growth and ultimate knowledge of who you truly are. Play all your cards. Let the world see them now before you get accustomed to hiding them.

These Boots Were Made for Walking

No, I'm not talking about walking out on or all over your lover . . . I'm referring to understanding that you are given everything you need to get where you need to go, including boots if that's a part of it. And, you have all the talent and gifts required for the Journey within you already. It is only resistance to truth and circumstances that hold anyone back from Dreams and rewards.

Think about your favorite pair of boots or shoes. They are likely either really cute or really comfortable or both. You just know you love them! Why? Because they fit you. They are a representation of who you are in that moment. In contrast, how about those trendy shoes you bought on a whim and only wore once because they really hurt your feet? Ouch! I've regretted wearing such killer shoes many times . . . usually about 40 minutes after putting them on. Off they fly, never to be worn again! Time to use what fits us and leave behind that which does not.

Freedom

Removing blister-rendering 4-inch heels is freedom in all its glory, but let's talk about another scenario—one that focuses on the inside a little more. You can't hold onto a butterfly for too long or she will wither and eventually die. The very small scales (powdery substance) that covers her begins to rub off, going with it her ability to fly, as well as her distinct coloring and beauty. This parallels how we allow others (or our own thoughts and beliefs) to hold us captive, keeping us from our true path. The longer this goes on, the more of our true beauty and ability wears off.

Obtaining freedom from such captivity is really about the "taking care of yourself" thing we talked about a few paragraphs up. Knowing what we truly need, and acting on that need, prevents anyone or anything from holding us back from our truth. Real freedom is understanding and living your truth. Anything short of this is life lived in a box. If I lived in a box all the time, I would have one hellacious attitude, which brings me to my next point . . .

No More Attitude . . . only Gratitude

We all have had non-serving attitudes with which we headed out the door, right? Well, the causes behind those tizzy fits were likely resistance related. We didn't like what just happened to us or what didn't happen for us. We resisted our truth. Changing our minds about these times is the key to freedom and to understanding the bigger picture of our Purpose, Dreams and Payoff. May I suggest attempting to be grateful for all that occurs in your life? This way you give yourself the opportunity to see the moments of your life as bridges to the next beautiful experience and not vicious monsters turned against you. Be thankful for all that is, and you will discover rewards beyond your wildest Dreams.

CHAPTER NINETEEN

The Physical Payoff

"To accomplish great things we must not only act, but also dream; not only plan, but also believe."
– ANATOLE FRANCE

The debilitating chronic migraine I told you about earlier stuck around for nearly thirteen years. At times, the pain even inched me to the edge of a cliff where I contemplated whether my life was worth living (suicidal life coach . . . another book). During those years, I resisted my circumstances, my state of mind, the root causes of my pain, and the possibility that it would ever change. This is my true definition of misery. I lived every day with the underlying thought that the next headache was just around the corner . . . and, it usually was. I created that reality.

It wasn't until I decided to do something different that I changed my circumstances. I drew a proverbial line in the sand and said, "Enough is enough!" Of course, I used more colorful language as I stood in my bathroom mirror and broke up with my chronic condition. That direct command to my body, my DNA, was the action that changed my life forever. That moment created the atmosphere—the very essence of change I needed to manifest my physical Payoff— something so simple, yet so profound. That's how it works in every area of your life. We have to do something different—something that breaks a cycle to discover the simple truth that gets buried beneath mounds of doubt, habits, comfort, and fear. I also know I would not have come to this place without the prerequisite of pursuit of Purpose and Dreams.

Awaiting Orders

Like a computer waits for you to tell it what to do and what you need, your body awaits orders to direct its next steps. Most of this order-presenting happens in the autonomic systems, but the kind I'm talking about occurs on a conscious level. During the period of chronic illness, I basically lived my life in opposition of my body. I especially hated the bouts of pain and depression that nearly stripped me of all joy and hope for my future. When I discovered that I no longer had to sit back and let my body be sick, that I could accept what had happened, be grateful and move on, I realized what truth and unabridged power we all possess to change our lives in all areas. The changes happened because I simply asked (okay, ordered with all my might) my body to do something different. I also believe that doing this while staring myself down in the mirror was an additional key that I should share with you. When we face ourselves, we come to terms with our state of being. We courageously accept all responsibility for our actions, beliefs, thoughts, and words. We grow up. We change.

I remember one other significant time when I commanded something while staring at myself in the mirror. A good friend of mine had been in a terrible accident and sustained a life-threatening head injury. She was on life support and was not expected to live. I got a call that the doctors were going to remove all support and let her go. For some reason, I just couldn't accept that it was her time to go, so I went to the mirror and pretended that I was her and commanded her to wake up and live! A mutual friend called that evening to tell me that she woke up just before they pulled the plug!

Is it possible that I became a surrogate for her in her broken state? This is a profound theory that gives substantial clout to the concept that we are truly all connected, don't you think? I believe that we have only just begun to understand just how linked we are and how able we are to bring life to each other. The possibilities are infinite.

Though you may never have experienced a miraculous healing or even close to it, you do have the power to change your body. I encourage you to experiment with this concept of giving orders to yourself on a daily basis. Get specific by asking for the change that will create health and joy. I started doing this daily and have experienced changes that I never thought possible. My eyesight is actually improving, and that just does not happen when you are past a certain age unless you get eye surgery.

Practice Often

This type of deep physical energy work is an exercise of sort, like stretching or muscle-building. You must practice it regularly in order to make real change and improvement. I keep a diary of my desires so I don't forget what specific areas to work on. My eyesight is one of those physical things I am developing on a molecular level by directing my DNA. And, it is changing before my eyes! If you are results-driven, like me, you will get excited about continuing this work and adding new body areas to your list.

The main point here is to explore the possibility that we are not helpless creatures with no control over our circumstances and our bodies. On the contrary, we are powerful beyond our comprehension, and that is why, for the most part, humanity has denied its divine ability to create and re-create life in this way. This is one of those moments where you are facing a concept—a theory that you must choose to embrace as your truth or not. You will ultimately either say, *"Yes, I believe it,"* or *"No, that is ridiculous, Kellie!"* But, I encourage you to at least try it out for a week or so and see if anything happens for you.

Your Body: The Energy Transformer

Just as our beings are influenced and ultimately changed by energy, they are able to release and expand that energy back into the universe. Each time you express an emotion or engage in some sort of energetic task, you present a unique energy signature with which other entities and matter intermingle. We live and breathe in a literal energy soup. Everything we do generates energy, a frequency, a charge that affects all that is. Spirit/Science expert, Gregg Braden, said in his book, *The Spontaneous Healing of Belief*, *"Experiments show that the focus of our attention changes reality itself and suggests that we live in an interactive universe."* If this is true, we can't help but change everything around us, in us, and connected to us. [Because] *"we live our lives based on what we believe about our world, ourselves, our capabilities, and our limits,"* [we must embrace new ideas, creating new beliefs, in order to experience something different in our physical world]. [Emphasis mine.]

Physical healing modalities, like Reiki, EFT, NLP, The Emotion Code, the laying on of hands, Reflexology, Homeopathy, and even Chiropractic all have one thing in common: they are all based on the movement of energy in and through the body. None of these practices are new and most are now highly respected by much of the world's population as being legitimate, effective techniques to improve health. However, there was a time when many of these practices were considered heresy, evil, and outside the normal way of life for most humans, so much so that religious groups and those in leadership tortured or assassinated anyone who practiced them—one of those "the earth is flat and we will all fall off the edge" moments. Isn't it interesting how far humans have evolved from previous beliefs? So, I guess it isn't such a stretch to believe that we have more energetic power than initially thought.

Elements of Desire

Physical Payoff manifests after a process that begins with desire. How long this progression takes is completely up to each of us. For some, it takes only a split second to see results and for some it takes years. Desire is tangible. It is creative in the way it can form, mold, and morph into reality. Dr. Steve G. Jones said, *"Desire constitutes the awareness of new possibilities."* Without it, there is nothing with which to work. What do you desire? And, are you willing to believe you already possess that desire? I hope so, because that is the only way to manifest it into the physical world. If you continue to want something, you push it off in the distance where it remains unreachable and elusive. **Wanting is fantasy. Belief is reality.** Think of your Dreams and desires as one or more of the four physical elements: Earth, Wind, Fire, and Water. If you can visualize them as already having substance, it's easier to believe that they already exist. This includes your desire to be healthy, whole, and vital.

It takes some practice to change the way you speak about your desires, let alone what you believe about them. How many times do you say, *"I wish I had a better income,"* or *"I want to be healthier,"* or *"That would nice, to have a new house."*? The Universe's action center yields to these statements of unbelief and will not move on your behalf. It wants to, but it hasn't received clear intention and orders from you. Remember how our bodies await orders? There is a seed there, but it hasn't been planted yet. It remains in a dormant state until you decide to plant it, water it, and cultivate it, believing it is already a beautiful flower or giant tree. In this moment of truth you realize that this type of manifestation can be applied to all areas of your life.

CHAPTER TWENTY

The Mind Payoff

"To enjoy good health, to bring true happiness to one's family, to bring peace to all, one must first discipline and control one's own mind. If a man can control his mind he can find the way to Enlightenment, and all wisdom and virtue will naturally come to him."

– BUDDHA

The day you wake up and realize your thought life reflects happy, serving, positive ideas is a day worth remembering for the rest of your life. This day is one that marks the most profound Payoff you will ever experience because it is the prerequisite to manifesting every Dream you've ever dared to imagine. And though this shift sometimes seems to happen overnight, it usually follows a long Journey of trial and error, failure, frustration, self-doubt, and limitations. Do, however, remember that your mind will continue to change and develop throughout your life. We never arrive at any one point where our cognizance says, *"OK, you're done! You have experienced your last new thought."*

We are in perpetual motion and a constant process of transformation, especially where our thought life is concerned. Each minute brings opportunity to expand, grow, believe, and embrace the next Dreams and visions for our lives. And though I believe in living in the present, it is okay to plan for the future with these grand visions. This is the state of mind that brings the Payoff in all the other areas (love, health, money, happiness). The mind makes all these blissful things reality when you get control of it, when you finally use it as a Dream Creator and not a vessel of worry and doubt.

You have to check how you are doing in this mental area often. Are you always thinking about what could have been or what bad things could happen? Do you dwell on the past or constantly dread the future? If so, you have not experienced the full Mind Payoff yet. That's okay. You will. Just keep practicing and making the adjustments to your thought life as needed. I won't tell you it's always easy when it's not. Most everyone on this planet has spent a lifetime with non-serving thinking patterns. Old habits change when you truly want them to change and when you believe in the change . . . not one second before.

Ending the Worry Game

Worry is like unwanted weight: you don't need or want it, and it only makes you unhealthy and less mobile. Yes, worry pins you down right where you are. Releasing it enables you to move freely to the next step or season of change. Most people don't realize how much it paralyzes them.

My husband lost his job recently and was forced to collect unemployment and begin searching for a new position. Though this situation was not ideal for our family and put a strain on our budget, I found myself without worry. I would not have been so calm and hopeful had I not spent much of my adult life experiencing the mudslides into which worry had thrown me (sort of learned my lesson). After extensive soul-searching, study, emotional healing, and mental practice, I realized that dread and imagining the worst case scenario did not serve me or my family. I changed my mind. I changed my life. And, no, my thought life is not perfect, but it's moved miles away from the gutter slime. Here are some of the activities that helped me.

Ten Anti-Worry Tips

1. Ask yourself this question: What is the worst thing that could happen? Answer yourself. Keep asking the same question until you are satisfied that you can survive the end result.

2. Write down or speak out what you are thankful for every day.

3. Focus on positive outcomes.

4. Speak about those positive things as though you already possess them, because you do.

5. Record yourself speaking about a situation you've been worrying about. Hearing your

Kellie R. Stone

negativity will remind you to make some changes in your vocabulary and thoughts.

6. Limit or discontinue the use of these words: but, could, would, should, can't, won't, isn't, not, didn't, don't, hate, never, haven't, blame, fault, regret, missed, defeat, impossible, improbable, dreadful, guilt, dislike, unworthy, wrong, bad, good, right, undeserving, limited, inadequate, worthless, stupid, dumb, ugly, scared, fearful, messed up, afraid, unloved.

7. When something concerns you, use comforting practices like prayer, meditation, journaling, grounding, protection spell, crystal or energy work, rest, massage therapy, counseling, coaching, or therapy.

8. Fill your mind and mouth with these action (fulfilling) words: doing, going, believing, acting, loving, moving, challenging, living, fulfilling, activating, generating, pushing, pulling, drawing, attracting, manifesting, changing, praying, meditating, connecting, training, growing, developing, healing, creating, bonding.

9. When you notice that your mind is wandering to non-serving thoughts and visions, quickly divert your attention to something you esteem as beautiful, loving, and joyful. Do this as soon as you can and before your thoughts generate strong emotions.

10. Realize that when you worry or fret over

162

something, your mind (coupled with genuine emotions) can and will make it real. The feelings you allow yourself to experience have energetic power even if the event hasn't actually happened in the physical realm. To your mind it's happening as it unfolds in your imagination. This is why visualization with focused emotions can manifest your Dreams. Remember, it works for the not so lovely things as well.

Quitting Is *NOT* an Option

One important thing I noticed that happened when I got my mind under control is that I suddenly stopped thinking about and using the option of quitting my Dreams and the activities that bring Payoff. A steadfast and bold new me emerged—a woman who follows through and does not take "no" for an answer. I make course corrections all the time, but that only makes me more determined to reach my goals, to live and fulfill my Purpose and claim my Payoff. I guarantee this is happening for you, too!

Dale Carnegie nailed it when he said, *"Most of the important things in the world have been accomplished by people who have kept on trying when there seemed to be no hope at all."* I believe he was talking about the mind, creating hope from desire and imagination. Consciously it is not seen or felt but is a tangible component of creative energy that works all around us and through us. Your imagination is a NOW event that is to be used in every moment of your life.

The Guardian of Now

I sat out on my deck one morning, listening to the birds tweet and the breeze flowing through my maple tree. Realizing how perfect that moment was, I pushed out invading thoughts and, though they were not wrong or bad, they threatened my perfect peace. The moment was profound in the sense it gave me a greater clarity about what it means to live in the now or present. This willingness to embrace each moment is something that will serve you as you re-calibrate your mind and go forward on the Journey to your ultimate Payoff—Love.

There have been moments of my life when I was so caught up in trying to analyze the past and plan for the future that I literally did not live my life in the moments that passed me like a speeding truck on the highway. The good news is that I stopped that cycle and so can you.

You may have already read hundreds of articles and books about living in the present but, somehow, like me, prior to my revelation, you did not receive the whole essence of those sacred writings. It's easy to learn about living in the now and even talk intelligently about it and not be practicing it. My world shifted when I became aware of my chronic distraction from the present. It's sort of like catching yourself dip into the cookie jar one too many times and saying to yourself, *"You don't need that."* It wasn't a guilt trip moment but a reminder to watch over my ship, to be the guardian of my now. Our authentic beings don't have identity in all of that garbage rolling around in our heads nor do they find it in the past or the future. No, identity lives in the now. No matter what we do to run from that fact, we will never escape the reality of how important each moment is to the fulfillment of our Dreams and Purpose.

Be the Guardian

In order to watch over and direct the mind and emotions, we have to appoint our true self as a guardian. She is who you want to be in charge . . . trust me. Her job is to simply watch and bring awareness to the fact that the past and future are invading the precious moments of life. I'm not saying that you can never think about the past or the future, it's just a balance of the three that culminate to create the perfect moment. And there is no other perfect time in your life than the moment in which you presently live. When we look to the past to relive those times we think were so great, we can bring on depression and sadness because of what we no longer have or can do. We lived those moments when they arrived, just as we live the one we are in. On the other end, when we look too much into the future, we may get stressed or anxious for what could be or what could not. You, as a guardian, will protect the mind from going into those traps.

Now Is Here for You

If you think about this present moment and ask yourself to analyze it for quality, I bet you will find no fault in it at all. If you do, then you are dipping into the cookie jar of the past or future. In other words, try not to compare the present with any past or future time. When I was chronically ill with the migraine headaches and other inflammation conditions, I would lay in bed and think about how much I wanted to be well, to run again . . . hell, to just clean my house. I would also think about how my life was before I got sick. I missed it. The combination of these times of walking away from my present caused a dark cloud to hover over my life. I began to believe I would never be whole, that my life was a sham—a mistake. How destructive those thoughts (my mind) were to my precious life. Living in the now is a way of life that you have to practice often to get really good at it. You may be tiptoeing around its banks and having glimpses of it here and there but, if you keep going there, you will discover a permanent lifestyle emerging. The present is always there for us. The past is past—the future is indefinite. Give the present a chance to prove how beautiful life is right now.

CHAPTER TWENTY-ONE

The Spirit Payoff

"There is no definition of beauty, but when you can see someone's spirit coming through, something unexplainable, that's beautiful to me."
– LIV TYLER

When the energy of the Universe draws you to your sacred Purpose, your soul engages and discovers all the beautiful, exciting moments you are meant to experience while here on Earth. This spiritual dance was spiraling even before the moment you were born and beheld the first light of day. We are innately driven to remember and find our creator and our sacred, authentic selves. Though this process is a long one, the more aware and open you become, the faster this connection happens.

This chapter is not about religion or to whom you pray but a nudge of encouragement to open your heart to all that life has to offer, including spiritual experiences beyond what you've allowed in the past. Living in a spiritual box can deteriorate human will and beauty from the inside out. I learned a long time ago to admit that I don't know everything and to embrace the possibility that there is always more to the picture. I now think, believe, and seek outside of my knowledge and constantly challenge what is presented as "truth." This is how I grow and remain open to life's adventures and Dreams.

The spirit Payoff is also one that is frequent and ongoing. As spiritual beings, we should experience a slice of enlightenment daily, and even by the moment. The best gift I gave to myself was the life-changing moment I accepted the profound connection between all life, sentient beings, all that was, is and will be, God, angels, masters, guides, and the elements of the Universe itself—a blessing beyond anything I'd ever experienced. This acceptance expanded Love within my being and answered many questions I had asked my whole life.

Sacred Purpose Revealed

While on my quest to define my Purpose, live my Dreams, and embrace my Payoff, I recognized the never ending circle of influence that continues to grow and pour into not only me but the Universe itself. Payoff reveals Purpose and Dreams just as clearly as Purpose and Dreams reveal Payoff. I love this! I only presented the three topics in the Purpose-Dreams-Payoff order because the linear mode is more easily grasped. One thing I've noticed is the more I submerge myself in the unknown of new spiritual challenges, the more my sacred Purpose opens up and is clarified.

Recently, I've been nudged to apply my energy-moving gifts in a greater way. Where I have always used intuition and even some forms of energy healing with clients and family, the call to do more has erupted within my own spiritual Payoff. This is a perfect example of how we can walk along, living our Purpose (or a part of it) and suddenly realize we have only skimmed the surface of a much deeper and richer plan. And, it is how you respond to these moments that directs your next steps. For me it was a greater sense of connection to everyone and everything that defined my Journey in a way I'd not clearly seen before. I consider this a sacred clue coming onto the scene. Embracing the spiritual Payoff and allowing yourself to grow with it enables you to recognize special clues and nudges when they do show up.

Transformation

You haven't seen your friend Rebecca for nearly a year. She looks completely different, with longer hair that's a new shade of red. She lost a good ten pounds or so, and she has a gigantic smile on her face that was not present 12 months ago during her divorce. Rebecca seems like a new person. However, if you had seen her every day of the past year she would not have suddenly been so different. It is this understated change that happens to us all a little at a time that causes us to not believe, at times, that we are growing or changing spiritually. We live with our experience, moods and gestures of faith and fear—all the daily changes. From that minute-to-minute perspective, the modifications are subtle and not usually significant enough to claim ourselves, let alone for anyone else to notice. Yet, consider what it would be like to have no contact with yourself for nearly a year (as with your friend). You would most definitely see a transformation if you had done the work and accepted spiritual challenge. My point is this: Believe in the process of transformation and realize it takes time and willingness to get outside of the box one step at a time.

Because spiritual change is the result of remembering who you truly are, the appearance of this transformation brings all those new facets of your Purpose to the surface. Your Dreams may even change to include things you never before considered, as Sharon expressed in her story. This is in no way giving up on your current Dreams but is enhancing them by giving you a clearer sense of your sacred identity. A new realm of possibilities opens up daily.

I recently dreamed that I was in charge of helping people recognize and activate their angels. I had never even thought about this being an actual job or necessary event. I figured that the angels just knew what they were supposed to be doing and just did it. Though I'm not really sure how profound the dream was to my actual spiritual Purpose, I am fascinated by how the suggestion opened my mind and heart to something new that I had never considered. This is how we expand ourselves. It all starts with a possibility.

Finding Peace

Spend five minutes on any social media site or watch

your local news broadcast and you'll understand that peace is something the world lacks, for the most part. Understand, though, lack of peace is not something you have to accept for yourself. In fact, living in the moments of your life, while pursuing Purpose, transforms unrest, violence, anger, remorse, depression, despair, anxiety, and hopelessness into pure peace. It's freedom from disturbance on all levels.

Of course, because we are now talking about spiritual Payoff, it is necessary to understand that peace is synonymous with reconciliation with yourself and how you fit into the big picture of life itself. This type of self-acceptance usually is not grasped from reading a couple of books or taking a course at the local college. Remember, there are Payoffs around every corner, behind every obstacle, with every experience. So, don't get discouraged if you have not reached your nirvana yet . . . most of us have not. Just keep practicing what you've learned. Dig deeper and find your personal peace. You will realize how far you've come out of the funky human state so unashamedly reported to us by those beautiful news anchors.

CHAPTER TWENTY-TWO

The Financial Payoff

"There is no way to prosperity, prosperity is the way."

— WAYNE DYER

I intentionally did not place this chapter at the beginning of the Payoff section because I wanted to remind you that money is not the only way we get "paid" for being who we are and living our Dreams and Purpose. Though I believe it is certainly an important part of our Journey, I generally do not focus all of my efforts in this area. In fact, when I took my attention off of making money, it began to flow into my life with greater ease. Funny how that happens! It's back to the concept that when you constantly need or want something, you push it away with an indirect denial of its existence in your life. When you say, "I want more money!" or "We need a bigger savings," you tell the Universe that you really haven't accepted that the finances are already yours to claim and receive. I know it's ass-backwards, but I've seen it work in my own life and the lives of countless other women entrepreneurs whom I highly respect. One of those beautiful souls is Lisa Marie Rosati. Her candid Payoff story is a prime example of how defining your Purpose, Dreaming big, and connecting to your truth moves mountains where Payoff is concerned.

Lisa Marie Rosati's Story

I remember when I first started working an online business model. It was a very exciting but confusing time. Like many women who decide to make a go of an online business doing their soul work, I subscribed to every free newsletter that interested me – which ended up being many! Go ahead, admit it . . . you've done it, too. Well, before I knew it, I had an inbox full of everyone's stuff and found myself even MORE CONFUSED. Whom did I help? How did I help? What was MY message? It felt impossible to hear my Inner Goddess whispering above the noise that surrounded me on a daily basis. I would spark what I thought was a great idea, and my immediate next thought would be . . . "Well, _____ does it another way, so maybe I should re-think this."

Monkey Mind . . . Inner Critic . . . Inner Bitch . . . all the same thing.

That looping thought process of second-guessing myself kept me stuck and, if that wasn't paralyzing enough, I knew deep down inside that I wasn't being completely authentic with my marketing message (and, by the way, the name of my first website was Create

<u>Authentic</u> Relationships!). I put a lot of time and energy into that website, I wrote an awesome eBook for my free gift, the website design was fabulous and chic looking, and my blog posts were informative and helpful but . . . there was something missing. The missing piece was my spiritual self—my truth.

A big part of me was separate from my work. As a matter of fact, I'll go as far as to say that my spiritual beliefs make up who I am, it's how I hold space in the world. I'm a Magical Practitioner and have been for my entire adult life. I live and breathe magic. My life is magic, and I view the world through a magical lens. ALL OF THAT YUMMY MAGIC was, of my own accord, consciously separated and hidden from the place from which I was conducting my soul work. Talk about incongruent.

I really should have known better. Thinking back, I probably did . . . but, I was so afraid. I feared that if I put up a website and proclaimed, "I'm a Goddess and so are you" that the world would fall over laughing at me! My ego simply would NOT allow it, so I kept it to myself for the first two years, until one day, during a mentoring session, it all came pouring out of me in the form of an epic meltdown. I could no longer hide my truth, my ego had to step down and I had to go for it.

Arriving at a place of acceptance, I realized that if people were going to laugh at me it would be less painful than continuing to live an in-authentic life. With every cell in my body, I

believe that I am a Goddess and that I am divine
in my very nature. I know that magic works, and
I know that getting into Universal flow is the
quickest way for a woman to create ease, grace,
abundance and joy (the Payoffs) in her life. I
couldn't keep that a secret any longer. I
absolutely had to share it. Like I said before, it
became too painful for me to continue denying
my magic professionally, so I had to consider a
change—a costly rebrand that would basically
put me back the entire two years I'd been
working to build my brand in the first place . . .
AND the money . . . oye!

I needed a whole new website, new graphics,
new blog posts, everything—the whole enchi-
lada. Not having the courage to come out into
the world in my authentic truth the first time
cost me a lot—a lot of time and a lot of money.

It was a lesson I will never forget.

I rebranded as The Goddess Lifestyle Plan. As
soon as I made a full body decision that "YES –
I am coming out of the Goddess closet loud and
proud," the Universe began aligning everything,
it all fell into place! My marketing message is
now so aligned with my soul purpose, it makes
my heart smile, and I sort of giggle every time I
say it.

My soul work is teaching spiritual women to
magically create an abundant life and business.

YAY! My truth!

I LOVE my truth, and I love the fact that I can

spend my days serving women in the most powerful and authentic ways. Stepping out into the world naked is a scary thing, I totally get it . . . but I have found that anything worth having usually scares the shit out of me!

Since stepping into my Magical Life and Business Mentor and Priestess work my brand has grown exponentially. I'm proud to say that I have a thriving global brand. One of my favorite magical principals is that once you send an intention out to the Universe, the Universe will help you manifest it. This is the same concept with your peeps (community and paying clients). Once you allow your authentic self to shine out from within you, the Universe connects you with the perfect people who need you . . . and then the abundance (Payoff) starts to flow in.

I've gotten so comfortable with being ME, that I decided to launch an extension of my Goddess Lifestyle Plan brand called Sugar Free Goddess, where I help women kick their carb and sugar addictions, lose weight and obtain optimal health. You see, being a carb-a-holic is my truth and, after many years of struggle, I figured out a way to have my cake and be healthy, too. So, I decided to share my methodology with the world, and it's been helping women everywhere!

I hope you've enjoyed reading about my journey. The take away of this story is to be yourself, completely and utterly YOU, in all of your unique-ness, quirky-ness and all that it means to be YOU. Speak your truth in life and in your

business. Work on being congruent so that you mean what you say and say what you mean. If you follow that formula, infinite success and prosperity will flow right to you . . . as if by magic.

It is truly inspiring to hear stories like Lisa Marie's that concur with the concept that being yourself, understanding your Purpose, and living it is the fastest way to any type of Payoff, including the money kind. These testimonies only solidify our need to rid ourselves of fear and self-doubt, revealing the Goddesses hiding in the closet.

Money Does Grow on Your Tree

I chose Wayne Dyer's quote *"There is no way to prosperity, prosperity is the way"* for this chapter because it simply states that prosperity is a way of life and not just something to enjoy in fleeting moments, weeks, or years. Consider yourself a human tree. You're a living entity that is basically governed by innate capabilities you have inside and out: It holds what you believe and what nourishment you or others contribute to your life. This human tree has an ideal plan—an optimal way—in which to grow and develop. This "plan" includes prosperity. I don't believe for one moment that (optimally) we were ever meant to live in lack or poverty. More importantly, I don't believe that we were meant to develop the mindset that enables such a life. We denied our roots somewhere along humanity's path . . . more like yanked them right out of

The Butterfly Payoff

the ground.

Dr. Dyer suggests that "prosperity is the way," and in doing so, he bombs our senses with a foundational (but oddly foreign) statement that is obviously more than just a passing fad to him. I define his statement as our prosperity is to our spiritual existence as water is to the planet. However, humanity has developed a twisted version of livelihood and how life itself is supposed to be lived: greed, popularity, the competitive edge, status, being right, and doing anything and everything to achieve have high-jacked our civilization. This pushes people over the edge of self-doubt and into the bog of I-don't-deserve-to-have-prosperity. In this template, the rich get richer and the poor get poorer. Our society will change when individuals change.

Prosperity Found

We have struggled for thousands of years to "make a living," ensuring survival. What if we were never meant to toil as we do? What if we were meant to simply live, grow, change, and bear fruit as a tree, or freely get paid for being ourselves like the butterfly? Prosperity is not having money, it's a mindset—the skeletal system of our existence that supports all that we Purpose to do. This concept is not what most of us have been programmed to believe. Changes in the current belief system need to be coaxed and supported by new information and a different kind of energy.

Robert T. Kiyosaki, author of *Rich Dad-Poor Dad*, explains, *"Emotions are what make us human. Make us real.*

179

The word 'emotion' stands for energy in motion. Be truthful about your emotions, and use your mind and emotions in your favor, not against yourself." And, though there is not one special way in which we are to find abundance (prosperity lifestyle), there are some things you can do to expedite change. Tied for first place with Kiyosaki's advice of using your mind and emotions is this: See the value in the goal and believe that change is worth it—a Payoff. What do you believe about money, finances, abundance, and prosperity? Answer this question honestly and you will discover why you are where you are concerning this area of life.

If you are like most, you likely have a potpourri of beliefs about how money is made, kept, spent, and saved. You may have always believed that money is difficult to come by and working hard is the only way to manifest it. Well, guess what? It *will* be all toil and trouble if that's what you believe. Even if you go through all the steps to chase your Dreams and life Purpose, without changing these limiting beliefs about money, you will struggle in that area. Hopefully, some of what we've discussed here will begin to take root and grow into a manifesting machine!

Truly changing your belief won't be as easy as just thinking you want to either. This rocking of your mind's boat requires time, practice, and constantly checking in with yourself. When you catch yourself speaking or thinking from the perspective of a broke woman, living in lack and perpetual struggle, do something to shock yourself. Yell, "NO!" Or pinch yourself . . . make it uncomfortable. You will then begin to associate this physical disturbance with poverty mentality. To move things along even faster, reward yourself for changing your thoughts and words before they create a non-serving situation in your bank account.

I still have to stay on top of my thinking and mouth regularly. It's too easy to slip back into old habits without standing guard. The process of swapping out old ideas, concepts, and beliefs will take at least as much dedication that you have given to solidify the ones you have now. If you are one of the lucky ones who have received abundance training from your family and mentors, I salute you. You already know who you are and how your mindset keeps you out of disbelief and scarcity. Now, your job is to take that glorious mindset of yours and get out there and teach others to find their prosperity!

Prosperity Shared

No human was ever meant to go hungry or sit out in the cold winter, shivering for lack of shelter or appropriate clothing. We've created this reality with a mutated sense of responsibility and love for all of mankind. There really is enough for us all, and there always has been. This is a call to wake up and understand what's really happening in our world and in our own hearts. Prosperity is for everyone. It may look differently for everyone, but the concept, as a whole, was meant for all humans. We have pressed our governments and leaders to practice and enforce equality where religion, sexual orientation, and race is

concerned, but we still watch millions of souls suffer daily without basic human needs. This crime proves how under developed we are as a society. We have a project before us, and you and I are on the creative team!

It starts with giving and sharing the elements of our own prosperity with others. I am doing it by writing this book, by leading a women's global community, by supporting people and organizations financially, by being who I am. It doesn't matter how you share yourself and your abundance, it's that you live the lifestyle of giving and mentoring in all that you do. If enough people do this, the world will change. All people will live with human rights intact. We will evolve as a society. The greatest gift you can give to this world is to define your Purpose, fulfill your Dreams, and live your Payoff!

Prosperity Lived

It's not difficult to know when you are in the presence of someone who lives prosperity. She speaks with joy and conviction. There is a distinct energy that fills the space in which she enters, whether it is a physical place, a phone connection, or a social media page. Spreading abundance of heart and substance is her way. She is none of us, and she is all of us—a connected, irreplaceable woman, living from her Purpose and Dreams. Don't envy her. Don't try to be her. Don't ignore her either. She has something we all need: Consistency. She carries her life with grace because she spent a long time believing in the steps, the change, the creation of her vision—all experiences that built the stairway to her Dreams.

Living prosperity takes you through some valleys, too. The trick is to feel the same joy and peace whether your bank account has a large number or not. That means no spouting off on your social media page about how broke you are all the time. It's consistently presenting loved-based emotions and decisions that kick fear to the curb (hear "What a Wonderful World" playing in the background all the time). That kind of energy ultimately translates into abundance. You do have a say in this process. Your life isn't some fishbowl experience dictated by outside forces. Take control in your mind, in your heart, in your spirit! If you do, you will live prosperity.

CHAPTER TWENTY-THREE

The Ultimate Payoff:
Knowing Yourself-Knowing Love

"Do you want me to tell you something really subversive? Love is everything it's cracked up to be. That's why people are so cynical about it . . . It really is worth fighting for, being brave for, risking everything for. And the trouble is, if you don't risk anything, you risk even more."

– ERICA JONG

Knowing yourself is a long-term investment of time, energy, and embracing your elements of darkness with the light. It is what happens when you focus on believing in your unique Purpose and the amazing Dreams that have been gently placed in your heart for this Journey. You are the master of your destiny, the artist who strokes the canvas with color, lines, and texture, creating a complete life painting. No one else can produce the exact same life that is solely meant for you. Comparing yourself to others and their accomplishments doesn't serve or bring the results for which you may have hoped. As far as I'm concerned, the only competition that's worth engaging in is the one you hold with yourself and your personal best.

Falling in love with the woman in the mirror is the single most satisfying relationship you will ever have. You may get angry with her, cuss at her, make fun of her, but she is still your number one—the love of your life. This self-adoration comes in a gradual process, though. There may or may not be an epiphany moment or a time when you just suddenly believe that you are your own best friend. More commonly it comes as a stream, trickling over rocks—subtle and ongoing.

I would beat myself up for making mistakes and not fulfilling what I thought I should. My heart cringed when I fell short or didn't achieve in various areas of my life. This only created more defeatists thinking and prolonged my state of self-destruction and sabotage. I hated my body, my scars, my inability to be well, and the lack of control I had over my life. This way of thinking tore small holes in my Dreams and hope for the future. And, as I described earlier, the moment of change did not come as a rushing tidal wave; instead, it moved in with grace and respect for my state of being. I learned to love my life, to be attentive to the woman I am right now, to understand that I'm enough just the way I am. That is where true Purpose lives and thrives.

Personal Relationships

With self-love and acceptance comes a strange and wonderful side-effect: You begin to give a deeper and more fulfilling love to others, and it returns with equal vigor. First of all, those to whom you are closest not only experience the results of changed actions and words but feel you shift energetically. Even if they can't quite figure out exactly what is different, others will respond to you in ways that maybe you have hoped for in the past. The energy of love trumps all other forms and finds its way into the most seemingly impossible cracks, crevices, and situations.

It's hard to reject love that pours in from the outside when the love you have for yourself is attracting it like a magnet. It's funny, however, to admit that we refuse this process at times, that we are unable or unwilling to respect and honor our mind, body, and spirit, as if our existence was some sort of science experiment gone wrong. None of us will ever be perfect with choosing self-love over the alternative self-doubt and denial of the magnificence we have within and all around us. But we can make more choices that serve who we are and who we desire to become. The Life-Journey is this if nothing else.

There is a saying that, to the best of my knowledge, has never been attributed to any one person but is powerful, nonetheless: *"Maybe the journey isn't so much about becoming anything. Maybe it's about un-becoming everything that isn't really you so you can be [and love] who you were meant to be in the first place."* I really believe this "un-becoming" is imperative for self-adoration to manifest. After all, we will never love ourselves completely until we peel away the layers that do not reflect our authentic beings and the truth that is represented there. And, in turn, relationships with all others find a more organic placement into life and Dreams.

Community

Zig Ziglar pioneered an iconic idea when he said, *"You can have everything in life that you want if you will just help enough other people get what they want."* The only way this happens is if you cultivate enough love in your life to overflow into your community. This willingness to help is not driven by greed or the need to show off or be seen but is the result of embracing your personal truth and the imperfection of your own life. We usually see and are able to meet the needs of others by recognizing our own weakness and owning the path we've chosen to progress to a more serving place.

There are always those who are ahead of you on this life Journey, and there are always those who follow steps behind. Opportunity to reach out to your community exists at all times and at every mile of the Journey. So, let there be no excuses like, *"I'm not experienced enough to help those people,"* or *"They will laugh at me because I'm not financially successful."* Nonsense! Get out there and be who you are right now! Someone, or lots of someones, need you and your message, your story, your gifts and your talents.

I had a vision during meditation once that gave me a bird's eye view of the world. Interestingly, however, I could perfectly see all the people, their faces, their hands, their smiles. Each person held the hands and feet of others, creating this chain-link grid that covered the entire planet. Its implication astounded me. This was true community—a connection to each other that could not be broken unless someone removed themselves from the grid. In addition to the web-like connection, there were spirals of light going to and from each person. These cords seemed to represent the contribution of each soul. Was I given this vision as an example of how our community, our world, is meant to function? No matter what it was or was not, I will never forget the beautiful picture of unhindered connectedness and love. I do see how it is possible to replicate the chain-link by offering ourselves to each other in service and compassion, by using our gifts out of a desire to see an advanced society immerge—one that is driven by peace, love, and the realization that we are one.

Changing the World

I truly believe there is a fierce women's movement happening on the planet today. This forward motion is driven by women just like you and me who desire change and a safe, blissful future for ourselves, our families, and generations to come. Though I support the idea of one woman bringing change to the planet, I've experienced how groups of women banding together, collaborating and fighting for truth, can multiply that change exponentially.

I encourage you to be a part of a women's group or cause that resonates with your deepest Dreams and Purpose. Even if all you can do is join a social media group or page and comment every once in a while, that's great! Start checking out other women's pages, blogs, websites, organizations, and books to get a feel for what is happening out there in other lives, communities, and cultures. And, if you can support women in business, please do so whenever possible. We have the ability to create a loving world environment that will ultimately be our planet's salvation.

Be Fierce
Fierce: Showing a heartfelt and powerful intensity

It's time to bring your heartfelt and powerful change to the world—the kind that gets noticed! First, *you* must see it, embrace it, and walk in it. Others will recognize it when you fully live it. What kind of change are you talking about, Kellie? Well, I'm referring to the releasing of limiting beliefs, healing of past wounds, the ending of self-sabotage, the setting of doable goals, the transformation of fear into faith, the execution of steps to fulfill your Dreams . . . anything that moves you closer to your Purpose and Dreams—basically, everything I've shared in this book.

How much more would you accomplish with a little fierceness . . . with a lot?

Can you imagine what it would be like to stare fear, procrastination, wishy-washiness, failure, excuses, illness, barriers, and poverty in the face and, with one fierce objective, say goodbye to them forever? The key to making it a reality is your intention. Wait . . . fierce intention! Heartfelt. Powerful. Intense. No, you can't just change the world by wishing you could or even saying you're going to. It's a deeper commitment than that. It's an I'm-going-to-do-this-or-starve-to-death kind of thing.

Picture a fierce tiger ready to catch that evening's meal. She is crouching low, muscles strong and ready, eyes on the target. Every outside element is noted but not distracting, she waits for the perfect time to strike. She is fierce and *WILL* get her meal. She saves her life and that of her family every time she executes this strength and inner drive to survive. I want you to think of executing what you've discovered here as that tiger thinks of her meal . . . a necessity.

Be Feminine

Try, for a moment, to envision what the planet would be like without women. First of all, the obvious would happen . . . extinction of our species. Well, what about feminine spirit? How important is it that we each embrace our unique feminine qualities and Purpose? I believe it is also imperative to the survival of our species and the progression of our society. Without the loving, intuitive, strong, mediating, empathetic, persuasive, creative, beautiful, and exhorting qualities of women, we would eventually exterminate ourselves. You can see the crucial times in which we live right now. It's a troubled world. But we have the feminine power to change it. Yes, you and I can band together with millions of other women to create change that saves lives and brings joy to the masses. It starts with you, deciding to change your own life enough to make a difference to those around you. As Margaret Thatcher once said, *"The woman's mission is not to enhance the masculine spirit, but to express the feminine; hers is not to preserve a man-made world, but to create a human world by the infusion of the feminine element into all of its activities."* It is *The Butterfly Payoff!*

Fight for Future

You hold weapons: love, peace, joy, hope, tolerance, empathy, and healing within yourself. And, with each passing day and life experience, you acquire more. You can either choose to hide your weapons or, with them, fight for our future. This fight is not the typical hot war zone battle, it's one fought by sharing yourself with others and doing so regularly. Your contribution to the world is a piece of the grand puzzle that will present a plan to overcome everything that hurts our world and threatens our continued existence.

Each generation welcomes warrior women who shake things up, let the pieces fall, and then put them all back together in an improved way. We are in this army. Our post is here and now—our lives, our connections, our Dreams. So, really, every time we don't succeed at fulfilling our own Dreams, we fail many. Have you ever thought about your life like this before? If not, try it. Start thinking about how you can make a difference, about how your Dreams connect to the bigger picture and the greater good of mankind.

One of my favorite quotes that epitomizes this kind of love is by Dr. Martin Luther King, Jr.: *"An individual has not started living until he [or she] can rise above the narrow confines of his [or her] individualistic concerns to the broader concerns of all humanity."*

Infinite possibilities

With each passing moment, you can choose to act, speak, and think from a place of either love or fear. Your future and that of our world depends on which one gets the most attention. The ideas represented in this book were hand-picked to lovingly guide you to a place where you are free to believe in infinite possibilities: the ultimate Payoff created with Love. Henry Drummond said it eloquently: *"You will find, as you look back upon your life, that the moments when you have truly lived are the moments when you have done things in the spirit of love."*

Imagine a world with no limitations other than those that its people believe in and live by. Guess what? We live in that world. Our only boundaries and hindrances to Dream-Fulfillment are those that exist in our minds. These are our ultimate beliefs that either propel us to victory and happiness or keep us in a state of doubt and frustration. It is solely up to each one of us to redefine what possibilities live in our world. The word *infinity* derives from Latin *infinitas*, meaning *"being without finish,"* which can be translated as "unboundedness." I get this picture of a woman suddenly freeing herself from wrist and ankle shackles because she just won't be put in chains and told she is done. And, although others contribute to the knowledge and strength we need to release ourselves from the chains of limiting belief, I believe the escape comes by our own will. We drop the chains by expanding ourselves daily and living within every moment of life we are blessed to breathe into.

Never allow someone else and their beliefs to define who you are or tell you something is impossible. Instead, choose to believe in yourself and your authentic Purpose fully, to execute it in a world that needs you right now. Author Sandra Kring spelled it out bluntly when she said, *"Unless someone can look into the core of your heart, and see the degree of your passion, or look into the depths of your soul and see the extent of your will, then they have no business telling you what you can or cannot achieve. Because, while they may know the odds, they do not know you. Nor do they know the power of your angels."*

I remember a time when I was around six-years-old. I had an amazing Schwinn bicycle that all the boys in the neighborhood wanted to ride. It was smaller than their ten speeds and could do tricks that were not possible on the larger big-wheeled models. One day I noticed they had made a ramp in the street and were frustrated when they couldn't do the things they wanted to with their bikes. One of the boys (the one I had a crush on) asked me if he could borrow my bike for the afternoon. *"You can watch,"* he said. I agreed, letting him take my purple baby across the street.

Boy, she could fly over that ramp! I was impressed with their tricks and how agile my wheels were. After about an hour, the boys said they had to leave and asked if I would watch their ramp but that I could not ride over it. "You can't do it because you're not strong enough, and, besides, you're a girl!" they mocked . . . even after I let them use my bike. As you can guess, I was furious and determined to show them a thing or two about being a girl with a cool bike. They left. I rode my bike over the ramp. I crashed. But it wasn't because of my lack of strength or that I was a girl. I later found out they had rigged the ramp so no one could safely ride over it in their absence. Yes, I got hurt, but I did not let those boys put me or my Dreams in chains. Even though I failed in the grand arena of bicycle stunts, I was proud that I tried, that I didn't base my actions on someone else's belief about my capabilities.

There is a distinct correlation between infinite possibilities and what we believe about ourselves. Even if you believe something amazing and profound can happen in the world doesn't mean you believe that you can or will have any part in that event. Insecurity in your ability tends to push the responsibility of greatness into the corner of someone else. A famous quote by Mahatma Gandhi comes to mind: *"You must be the change you want to see in the world."* If certain things seem unfair and out of balance to you, it's because *YOU* have been given the insight to recognize those discrepancies and the gifts and heart to do something about them. The only thing that stands in your way to creating change and executing infinite possibilities is your belief in yourself and your potential.

Remember I told you that I stopped saying "I want or need this and that" because it felt that in some deep way I was proclaiming that I wouldn't have this thing or I didn't really believe I could have it. Instead, I now say this: "I see and believe that those things are either already here or are on their way." The energy is different. It's like walking through the door to a Dream that's unfolding just beyond the threshold instead of just staring at the wood barrier, hoping I might get to see what's happening on the other side. This mental change takes time and practice to fully embrace as an automatic response to your life and Dreams. Do I slip up and limit myself? Yes, of course. And you will, too.

No matter where you are on your Journey, you will—if you haven't already—understand that the true connection to love and peace is a simple act: Gratitude. We can read all the books we want, and we can even apply all that we've learned from the pages of wisdom and experience but, without the spirit of thankfulness, we won't enter into the realm of ultimate truth and enlightenment. Everything that happens in our lives occurs because of some other action before it. I don't know about you, but I choose to be thankful for all that is. This emotion connects me to love and removes the judgment factor that so often can throw a minimally disruptive situation into a really hot fire. As we come to the end of this book, I see your life changing dramatically if you simply apply just this one principle. Be grateful . . . always.

Believing that our lives are a part of our universe in a fully integrated realm of possibility creates the kind of hope and Dreams from which miracles and ultimate love flows. When you are grateful and understand that you are not alone in your endeavors, that you have all you need within, that every step you take has meaning and Purpose, you stop second-guessing yourself and life. Calmness resides in you, around you, and pours from you—peace that becomes the foundation of all you do, say, think, and believe. From this source of peace your Purpose is defined, everything you've ever dreamed of can be reality, and the Payoff is priceless.

"The only way to come into my true form,
my true colors,
is to go through the process of transformation.
Because of it,
I am bold.
And, it is in my willingness to be fragile,
that the strength of my being comes forward."
                                    –CATHY LYNN

"May the wings of the butterfly kiss the sun,
and find your shoulder to light on.
To bring you luck, happiness and riches today,
tomorrow and beyond."

—KHANDRO

Kellie R. Stone
Author

From early on, my heart told me that everything I would experience in my life, from the people I would meet to the heartbreak and trauma I would experience was to prepare me for living my purpose. During my darkest days (yes, I've had them, too) I would remember those heart messages (more like resounding calls from a bullhorn!) Like many women, I would ask—okay scream out the question "Why me?" as I swam through a melting pot of trauma, divorce, loss, chronic illness & self-sabotage, which I now see was leading me to the dynamic work I now do today with women. Each experience empowered me to draw out the lessons and character traits I needed on my own sacred inner journey (which continues today) and to step fully into my role as a Women's Life-Purpose Visionary and Inner Journey Strategist.

Today, I stand before you and all women with a message of truth and authenticity. I LOVE who I am today, and you can, too, love yourself! My deepest dream is for every woman to discover, own and bring forth her unique reason for being here and embark on an inner journey that serves her unique purpose. I am here to guide you on your sacred inner journey and help you emerge above and beyond whatever holds you back from realizing your own dreams. I am guided by a deep spiritual connection to God and Universal energy, my own intuitions, and by the tools and knowledge I've collected along the way. It is with these influences that I'm now able to lead women to fulfilled dreams and an authentic life filled with creativity, hope, joy, and success.

Love and Peace,
Kellie

On her quest to be a sacred guide for women on their journey of self-discovery, Kellie is an avid student of life. She is not only the founder of the global women's community, Women's LifeLink, but works privately with clients as a Women's Life Purpose Visionary, Inner Journey Strategist, Intuitive Reader and Energy Healing Practitioner. Kellie received her coaching certification through renowned spiritual life and business coach, Karen Coffey and the Hope of Humanity Foundation and her Reiki attunement through Reiki Master, Christine McKenna Eartheart. Though she no longer serves in a pastoral capacity, she was also ordained as a Journey Pastor and Youth Minister in her hometown of Indianapolis.

Kellie's published articles:

Womenslifelink.com
Livestrong.com
Allthingschic.com
Timefindersmagazine.com
Coffeytalk.com
Goddesslifestyleplan.com
EmpoweredWomanMagazine.com
and many other blogs and e-zines.

Other books by Kellie R. Stone:
Are You out of Your Freakin' Mind?
Break Mental Barriers and Live from
Your Sacred Creative Space

Co-author of the International
Best Seller:
Success In Beauty: The Secrets to
Effortless Fulfillment and Happiness

Connect with Kellie at:
WomensLifeLink.com
WomensLifeLink@gmail.com.

Lisa Marie Rosati
Contributing Author

Passionista and Visionary Lisa Marie Rosati is a renowned Inner Goddess Catalyst for women, Creatrix of The Goddess Lifestyle Plan + Sugar Free Goddess + Smithtown Weight Loss and co-author of the international best-selling books – *Embracing Your Authentic Self* and *In Pursuit of the Divine*. Lisa mentors women around the world on how to become a Modern Day Goddess by consciously designing how to get their health back, balance their feminine and masculine energies, ignite the fire within their souls and live a luscious goddess life filled with passion, radiant health, entrepreneurial success and prosperity.

Lisa's unique combination of strategic thinking, laser

sharp intuition, vast knowledge of holistic health, psychology, human behavior, healing modalities and women's spirituality, plus 20+ years of metaphysical study and practice, results in an effective mix of spirituality and "real world," no-nonsense practicality that supports her private clients in embracing their own Inner Goddess.

Lisa serves a global audience of women as an Expert Columnist with Aspire Magazine, a Dietetics & Nutrition Expert for sharecare.com, and as a sought after speaker. While running her 3 businesses + raising 3 children, Lisa exemplifies the Goddess Lifestyle as she embraces her sensual and powerful feminine nature with pride and encourages other women to do the same.

Visit Lisa Marie at:

GoddessLifestylePlan.com

Jan Deelstra
Contributing Author

Self-Esteem Specialist, Jan Deelstra, is the trans-
formational author of: *Blessings in the Mire: A True Story
of Miracles & Recollections, Escaping the Chrysalis:
Introduction to Gestalt Techniques for Self-Esteem
Transformation, The Flying Game, Shadows Attached: Mad
Woman Poetry volume 1*, and *Infinite Pie*. Jan's Motto:
Gestalt means whole and so are you.

Her life's calling is to help others transform into the
greatest version of themselves, using self-esteem-
bolstering gestalt techniques, including dream analysis

and hot-seat work.

With a background in social issues, Deelstra has championed diverse populations, including working to provide gestalt therapy techniques to marginalized members of society. She worked for over ten years at the Department of Human Services in varied positions, offering self-sufficiency classes and counseling to adolescent parents, and to single mothers receiving public assistance. She also worked as a Graduate Student internship placement supervisor to students studying social work.

Realizing that true social change begins inside, Deelstra is committed to improving the lives of others. She teaches and writes in the vein of gestalt self-awareness, and bridges the waters of psychology and metaphysics. An avid reader and writer, Deelstra has written for children, adolescents, and adults, and is currently editing her latest book, working title Gestalt Techniques for Wellness, due out in early spring 2015.

Correspondence welcomed:
JanDeelstra@JanDeelstra.com

Play in her garden:
JanDeelstra.com

Sharon Nicholas
Contributing Author

Sharon Nicholas is the Publisher of Empowered Woman Magazine that released its first issue in January of 2014, Co-host of Empowered Woman Radio and Co-founder of The Word of Mom Network.

As an online publisher, her blogs Networking WAHM and Moms Indulgence flourished. Nicholas grew as a writer and later began to Co-host and guest Co-host on various radio shows.

Nicholas has held a number of positions in various fields, including the Hospitality, Telecommunications,

Insurance and Software fields. Today, she's the President and Publisher of Empowered Woman Magazine. Prior to starting the magazine, Nicholas founded the Tourette Syndrome ~ Awareness Movement. She is currently a contributor to Faith, Hope and Love and a consultant to Sing Project Records.

Visit Sharon at:

EmpoweredWomanMagazine.com

Alexa Linton
Contributing Author

A modern day cowgirl with a mission, Alexa Linton is known for lighting up her world and her clients with her infectious personality, bold coaching style and her secret sauce: the Body Talk System. When these forces combine, perceptions transform forever, and health and lives change irrevocably in the most fabulous ways. With over ten years of experience working with horses as an Equine Sport Therapist, as well as thousands of animals and people, Alexa has developed a healing style that is as intuitive as it is inspiring. Her first and foremost priority is results, and she has been a catalyst for positive and lasting change for thousands as a practitioner, teacher and author.

A fire-starter by nature, there is nothing Alexa loves more than seeing people light up from within and their lives change "magically and miraculously" as a result. Well, that and animals. Alexa's animals are a big part of her healing team, providing insight, giggles, massages and the effect of the perfect furry hot-water bottle. Except for her mare Diva, of course, who is much too large to be a hot water bottle, and prefers to rocket people into powerful transformation with her own style of Equine Facilitated Light up. It is Alexa's big mission to help people find the fire in their relationships, career and bodies and truly live a life they love.

Visit Alexa at:

AlexaLinton.com

TheDivaProject.ca

alexa@alexalinton.com

Charlotte Howard
Contributing Author

The Beauty Confidence Guru, Charlotte Howard, is a renowned Transformational Life Coach for Women, Award-Winning Hair Artist, Founder of Hair Artist Association, Founding Premier Member of Women Speakers Association, Success & Beauty Talk Radio Host, Publisher of Hair Artist Lifestyle Magazine, Creator of Heart Centered Women Publishing and five-time Best Selling Author.

Charlotte's mission is to empower millions of women to discover fulfillment and happiness in their lives. She is all about women empowering women to create a renewed sense of energy and motivation for enhancing themselves, lives and business from the inside out!

Charlotte's unique ability is getting women to take immediate action on creating fulfillment and happiness, using a heart-centered systematic approach to produce impeccable results, in record time. She's dedicated her life to empowering women to touch the lives of others, adding value to people's lives in an authentic way and creating life changing breakthroughs by enhancing their mind, body and soul.

Charlotte's key message: "Each of us has a personal calling that's as unique as a fingerprint – and that the best way to succeed is to discover what you love and then find a way to offer it to others to make their lives better."

This entrepreneur and single, busy mom of four resides in South Carolina with her family. During her free time, she loves to indulge in spa & beauty treatments, massages, travel, cooking, reading, writing, walking and movies.

Connect with Charlotte at:
TheHairArtistAssociation.org
CharlotteHowardInfo.com

Cathy Lynn
Contributing Artist

I believe that everyone needs to have a strong sense and love of self. I believe that everyone deserves to know themselves in such a glorious way that being in their own company, alone, is uplifting. I believe that everyone deserves a slice of their life that is theirs and theirs alone. I believe having all these things makes people more interesting but, most importantly, I believe having all these things makes people happier.

Cathy Lynn is a writer, facilitator and artist. In her day job, she's an executive. She's written for the personal growth blogs 3 Shared Paths and Women's Life Link.

She is co-owner of Inkwell Basics and is owner of The Barefoot Farm. She lives somewhere between the city and the country with her princess cat, Menzie.

Bibliography

Braden, Gregg. *The Spontaneous Healing of Belief: Shattering the Paradigm of False Limits.* Carlsbad, CA: Hay House, 2008. Print.

"Butterfly Lore." *Baylor University || Lake Waco Wetland ||.* N.p., n.d. Web. 06 June 2014.

"Find the Famous Quotes You Need, ThinkExist.com Quotations." *Thinkexist.com.*

ThinkExist, n.d. Web. 06 June 2014.

Folsom, William. *The Art and Science of Butterfly Photography.* Buffalo, NY: Amherst Media, 2000. Print.

Kryon, and Lee Carroll. *The Twelve Layers of DNA: An Esoteric Study of the Mastery within.* Sedona, AZ: Platinum Pub. House, 2010. Print.

Moore, Steve. *The Dream Cycle: Leveraging the Power of Personal Growth.* Indianapolis, IN: Wesleyan Pub. House, 2004. Print.

Nielsen, Kim E. *Beyond the Miracle Worker: The Remarkable Life of Anne Sullivan Macy and Her Extraordinary Friendship with Helen Keller.* Boston: Beacon, 2009. Print.

Tolle, Eckhart. *A New Earth: Awakening to Your Life's Purpose.* New York: Plume, 2006. Print.

Bibliography

Tolle, Eckhart. *The Power of Now: A Guide to Spiritual Enlightenment.* Novato, CA: New World Library, 1999. Print

Walsch, Neale Donald. *Conversations with God.* Bath: Camden, 2004. Print.

Williamson, Marianne. *A Return to Love: Reflections on the Principles of a Course in Miracles.* New York, NY: HarperCollins, 1992. Print.

"Women's Life Link Creating a better world . . . one woman at a time." *Women's Life Link.* N.p., n.d. Web. 06 June 2014.